"Nearly every pastor I have ever met is, like me, far better with the Bible and people than with the organizational aspects of ministry leadership. We are certain to get burned out, used up, frustrated, and discouraged because what we cannot do threatens to undermine everything we are trying to do. What we do not know is not taught in a theology class, written about in a Bible commentary, or modeled in virtually any church. Some of us grind it out, wasting energy and resources. Some of us just break one way or another and never recover. Some of us quit the ministry and walk away, forever jaded. Still others of us cannot find a job outside of ministry, and so we go through the motions pretending to care, cashing our check and reducing a divine calling to yet another job.

But a few of us get an executive pastor who is strong where we are weak, clear-sighted where we are blind, glad to let us do what we are good at, and build a team to do the rest. The guys like me need to read this book and pray for a guy like that to help them. The guys like that need to read this book and pray for a guy like me who needs help. I was a guy who was about ready to preach his own funeral before Pastor Sutton and Pastor Dave joined me as the executive elders at Mars Hill Church. Praise God for guys like that."

MARK DRISCOLL
Founding and Lead Pastor of Mars Hill Church, Cofounder of Acts 29 Church Planting Network, Founder of Resurgence, *New York Times* #1 Best-Selling Author—and guy who sucks at organizing it all

"The church is not a business. But there is no denying that it conducts business and needs to be organized. That's where Sutton Turner comes in. He offers a candid, motivating, and practical look at what happens when those with experience, expertise, and success in the business world decide to become servant leaders and come alongside pastors who are often gifted as preachers and visionaries but unprepared or overwhelmed by the organizational needs of a growing and thriving ministry."

LARRY OSBORNE
Author and Pastor, North Coast Church, Vista, CA

"This book will challenge you to invest your life in the greatest cause of all—the kingdom of God. Sutton describes with great transparency the journey God led him on—from being a successful entrepreneur to discovering significance in living for and serving a higher purpose. This is also one of the very few books that offer practical insight into the role of the executive serving their local church. When I served as an executive pastor, there was no training manual or guidebook to help me. It's no surprise, knowing Sutton, that he would dedicate this book to help current XPs and those who could one day find themselves in this role. He is one of the most thoughtful and generous leaders I know and models the message of this book not only in his life and relationships, but also in the way he serves his pastor and church. My prayer is that it will inspire you to invest your life in the greatest and most fulfilling roles—partnering with Jesus as he builds his church."

DAVID BRANKER
Pastor, Celebration Church, Jacksonville, FL

"As a marketing director in a Fortune 50 global company, sorting out God's call to pursue volunteer eldership required diligent prayer and study. Pastor Sutton has now provided a biblical approach for anyone sorting through a similar desire to faithfully serve Jesus' church primarily with gifts of administration and leadership. *Invest* is packed with wisdom gleaned from shepherding two of the fastest growing churches in the United States. With a balance of theological and practical wisdom, Pastor Sutton has provided a blueprint for volunteer elders to provide faithful leadership, stewarding the time, talent, and treasures God has entrusted them to pursue his mission."

MATT ROGERS
Director, Microsoft Corporation, and Nonpaid Elder, Mars Hill Church, Seattle, WA

"God is calling men to come alongside pastors and invest their gifts for the kingdom. Sutton Turner's *Invest: Your Gifts for His Mission* serves as an amazing tool that will assist these men to catch a vision for life as an executive pastor."

MIKE BUSTER
Executive Pastor, Prestonwood Baptist, Plano, TX

"I can attest to you from personal experience and from knowing many executive pastors like Sutton through the years that making the leap from the business world to investing more fully in God's kingdom is an incredibly fulfilling and rewarding adventure, despite the cost in worldly terms. I ask you to read this book and to consider carefully—with an eternal perspective—what you could *get to do* if you accepted Sutton's invitation."

DAVID LONSBERRY
Executive Director, Business & Finance, Christ Fellowship, West Palm Beach, FL

"Sutton invites other men to be executive pastors, to use their business skills to sharpen the church, serve senior pastors, and serve Christ. There is no dichotomy between sacred and secular, as all of our gifts and abilities can be used for Christ's church."

DAVID FLETCHER
Founder, XPastor.org

"*Invest: Your Gifts for His Mission* is a great resource for both senior pastors and kingdom-minded business leaders. Sutton does a great job of explaining how valuable the relationship is between kings and priests. Simply put, this is a must read that will lead to unparalleled results!"

MARC CLEARY
VP of Development, Association of Related Churches (ARC)

"The harvest is ripe, but the laborers are few. Jesus has called us to work and bring in the harvest of souls, and I would argue that our work or job should be in line with the skills and talents that we have. Sutton has lived the life that he encourages all Christians in business to live. I have watched him use his gifts to run his business in Texas, expand his skill set at Harvard, manage business in the Middle East, and bring all of his skills to serve as an executive pastor for Mars Hill Church. Sutton has been a living example to me of how my gifts and talents can help benefit the house of God. I pray that we can change the world for his glory and help build the local church with the same tenacity and fervor that we build our businesses."

COREY BELL
Entrepreneur

"If you have ever felt the tug to move from success to significance, you should devour this book. Sutton has written a practical guide on how God often times takes successful men and uses them to make an eternal kingdom impact. I believe God may use this book to change the course of your life. Read at your own risk!"

ASHLEY WOOLDRIDGE
Executive Pastor, Christ's Church of the Valley, Phoenix, AZ

"Sutton Turner is a remarkably creative, out-of-the-box thinker and 'doer of the Word.' He always brings seasoned leadership and real-world know-how to everything that comes his way in ministry, in business, and in life. Need a fresh jolt of inspiration and intellect? Sutton delivers both in his newest book *Invest: Your Gifts for His Mission*. A must-read for all who want to go to the next-level while using their God-given gifts to accomplish his plan for their life."

DAVID O. MIDDLEBROOK
Founding Shareholder, Church Law Group

"The need for leaders gifted in business to use those gifts in the church has never been greater. Church administration and financial issues have become increasingly complex. As my friend Sutton says in this insightful book, 'The church is a family, not a business.' But every family must handle business issues and 'the larger the family, the more complicated the business.' I pray this book will cause many to consider the calling to strengthen their lead pastors and help their churches reach more people with the gospel by serving as executive pastors."

TROY ANDERSON, JD
Executive Pastor, Operations & General Counsel, The City Church, Seattle, WA

"Sutton Turner has made a significant contribution to ministry with this work. The honesty, insight, and encouragement relayed in *Invest: Your Gifts for His Mission* will stir up passions among senior pastors, executive pastors, and potential executive pastors to more fully leverage people and their gifts to accelerate the advancement of God's kingdom."

DAVID ANDERSON
President of LearnToLead and Author of *How to Run Your Business by THE BOOK*

"Sutton has done a masterful job of conveying the scope of work required at the executive level in the local church and the heart required to act in that role. His personal account is authentic, challenging, and inspirational. If you feel that God is nudging you to use your business skills in his kingdom, but you don't know how that could possibly work for you, you should read Sutton's book."

RICK HOLLIDAY
Executive Director, North Point Ministries, Atlanta, GA

"Sutton Turner is a friend and someone with a burning passion to see the church extended across the earth and fulfill all her God-given potential. He has a unique skill set that affords him a dynamic leadership perspective on what it takes to build an effective organisation. I highly recommend this book if you want your church to make an impact and have influence."

GRANT THOMSON
Global Marketing Director, Hillsong Church, Sydney, Australia

"If you have the gift of leadership, a knack for business, and enjoy seeing organizations operate efficiently, you may be the person God uses to impact thousands of lives. Through the words of his book *Invest: Your Gifts for His Mission*, Sutton Turner unpacks his life journey in a way that will leave you challenged to evaluate your calling. Take the time to read the very helpful tool that will hopefully change more than just your life!"

JASON WILSON
Executive Pastor, NewSpring Church, Anderson, SC

"Charles Spurgeon wrote, 'It takes more skill than I can tell to play the second fiddle well!' Whether you sit in the first or second chair, great grace and the calling of God is required equally for both. Sutton's book on this topic is a strong challenge to laymen in the church to consider how God may be leading them into a more significant place of service. If you are a serious man of God, if you'd like to apply your business acumen for kingdom work, if you desire to come alongside pastors and leaders and provide practical wisdom and skill to ensure greater outcomes in ministry, then I say, read on!"

JOHN COLLINS
Executive Pastor, Harvest Christian Fellowship, Riverside, CA

"My friend Sutton Turner's book *Invest: Your Gifts for His Mission* is a masterpiece. Not many books have been written on being and succeeding as the second chair, never mind one that is engaging, honest, helpful, respectful, practical, and, most importantly, biblical. Using his own life experiences, Sutton gives all of us insight into servanthood and the rewards of a life filled with integrity. Every pastor, no matter how small or big the church, every faith-based business person, no matter how small or big their influence, needs to read and apply this book."

TOM ATEMA
President & Founder of Vertical Horizons Group and Author of *Leadership in Blue Jeans*

"After 12 years in the corporate world, I made a shift into full-time ministry to help my former youth pastor, Chris Hodges, plant Church of the Highlands in Birmingham, Alabama, in 2001. I had no idea how much my business background would help me add value to our church. Pastor Sutton does a fantastic job in this book painting a picture of what this transition can look like as well as how effective you can be for the kingdom. There is great wisdom found in his story, along with application for yours."

LAYNE SCHRANZ
Executive Pastor, Church of the Highlands, Birmingham, AL

INVEST

YOUR GIFTS FOR HIS MISSION

SUTTON TURNER

FOREWORD BY PASTOR MARK DRISCOLL

19   18   17   16   15   14   13
7   6   5   4   3   2   1

We all invest our lives in something or someone. From one business-savvy brother to another, the best investment decision you can make is investing your gifts for Jesus' mission by serving him, his church, and a lead pastor.

PASTOR SUTTON

Acknowledgements

I FIRST WANT TO THANK my incredible wife, Marci Turner. As you will read in chapter one, she should have packed her bags in the late 1990s when she realized I was not a Christian, but she did not. Instead, she stayed and prayed Jesus would save me. She is my best friend and the person I am blessed to spend the rest of my life with.

I also want to thank Mark Airhart. Since 1997 he has been a friend and mentor. He has shown me what a great family looks like and how to have an incredible friendship with your grown kids based on unconditional love. I will never forget the time we spent together working in the Middle East.

Thank you to Pastor Mark Driscoll and Pastor Dave Bruskas. These last years have been very challenging, but their friendship and our laughter together has made it fun. I look forward with joy to our shared future.

During my years in the Middle East, I had the great opportunity to work with Abubaker al Kouri, Abdulla al Qamzi, and Khalid al Mannai. I thank them for their friendship and the leadership lessons learned while working with them.

Finally, I am thankful to work with Jonathan Brodhagen and Andrew Myers. This book would not have been possible without their support and assistance.

Table of Contents

Foreword

ONE OF MY GRANDFATHERS was a red potato farmer. The other was a diesel mechanic. My dad was a construction worker. Jesus saved me in college while studying communication. My family can change their own oil but not organize a profit-and-loss statement. I made it through college without a clue on anything related to money, stewardship, or organizational structuring.

Sensing a call to ministry, I started studying the Bible intently. I read big books with footnotes and enjoyed it. I got married in college, then graduated. Eventually, I interned at a church and then planted my own church while pursuing a master's degree in theology. I started an organization and got an MA, still without any clue about the practical side of leadership and working *on* an organization, not just *in* one. It's a miracle I did not end up doing prison ministry from the inside.

As the years rolled on, my ability to preach and teach the Bible grew. My ability to pastor people grew. But my ability to run an organization did not. I did not know how to deal with issues such as fundraising, real estate, organizing people, cash flow, payroll, budgeting, legalities—pretty much anything not clearly in the Bible or dealing with a sinful or suffering person. I was totally unprepared for more than half of ministry. And as our ministry grew, things got worse and worse. As our church grew, I just worked harder. At one point, I had over twenty direct reports, an intestinal ulcer, blown adrenal glands, and my body was so burned I literally could not stop working and fall asleep. I was about ready to stop talking about Jesus and just go to heaven to talk with him. I was in my thirties, and old men felt sorry for me.

In high school, I played football and baseball with a guy who diligently hit the weight room day after day and only worked on his upper body. He literally never worked his legs. Eventually his upper body looked like an action figure and his lower body looked like a set of chopsticks. One day, I literally watched the guy fall over for no reason. He was completely out of balance.

When it came to leadership, I was like that. And since organizations tend to reflect the strengths and weaknesses of their leaders, our church was like that. To make matters worse, since like attracts like, I ended up with a bunch of leaders who were like me. Lots of people who wanted to write, preach, teach, and debate theology, but nothing but skinny legs when it came to anything else. We could debate theology with nerdtastic skill, but good luck finding an org chart or spreadsheet saying how many days of cash we had on hand.

I am a prophet. I preach, teach, write. Prophets attract a crowd.

Priests then step up to love and serve the crowd. But unless a king shows up, the big crowd is just a big mess. We were a big mess— a Bible-believing, Jesus-serving, church-planting, convert-making, media-garnering mess. And we were about ready to fall over if we did not start working our legs.

In God's grace, the King of kings sent us some kings. We don't have it all together, but we are working our legs.

In reading this, most pastors will think something like, "Thankfully, I'm not like Mark." Most pastors are just like me. They are just in denial. If ministry fails, most pastors will not be taking jobs as a CEO, CFO, COO, or leading a division such as marketing or sales for a large company.

Most will become counselors, teachers, and give their life to people and/or ideas somewhere down the food chain in a large organization.

We need help. We don't need more people like us in leadership. We need people with experience that is different from ours, skills that are different from ours, and education that varies from ours. We need to be humble enough to admit that just because we get to teach the Bible for a living doesn't mean we do not also have a lot to learn—and some of it is from the general revelation and common grace that the Bible tells us to also learn from. The rest is littered in the Scriptures, in places like Proverbs and Jesus' parables on stewardship. And while we will do fine exegeting the Hebrew and Greek text, we are more likely to walk on water than translate those principles into organizational action.

Dear Bible Guy, please don't be yet another nerd who proof texts verses on lovers of money, lording it over like the Gentiles with curse words like "pragmatism" and "it's all about the numbers" criticisms. Stop using God's word as a defense to keep working the upper body and ignoring the legs. Your church body needs some legs just like ours.

I'm deeply thankful for Pastor Sutton and his gifts. He's being pretty humble in this book. He's a Joseph sent as the former CEO to run an empire for a sheik. Our little church is like t-ball for Babe Ruth. But he loves Jesus, me, the church, and our people. He's helped a ton. He's helping us get our legs. And if the guys like me would take counsel from guys like him to heart, the King of kings might even send them a king to multiply the vision God has given them, thanks to some legs built for a good hard run up the next hill.

Pastor Mark Driscoll, Founding, Preaching & Vision Pastor
MARS HILL CHURCH, SEATTLE

I WISH I HAD MET Sutton Turner fifteen years ago when I was launching a church plant in Albuquerque, New Mexico. Even better, I wish he had been my very first staff hire. Here's why: next to an effective preaching ministry in the church, nothing is more important than good stewardship, and Sutton Turner is the most gifted steward I have met in my twenty years of ministry experience.

As you read this book, you will understand that stewardship is a common theme in the Bible and encompasses much more than just money. As church leaders, we are called to be good stewards of the resources Jesus provides for us. We are entrusted with money, time, and people in order to fulfill the mission he has given us. Or as we like to say at Mars Hill Church, we are given time, treasure, and talent to steward while on mission with Jesus.

The most valuable and powerful gift in this triad is talent: people possessing supernatural abilities endowed by the Holy

Spirit to be exercised in serving others. And if this is true, then one of the most critical roles in church leadership is the organization and mobilization of this greatest resource: people. People must be in the right place at the right time, with the right skills and the right assignments for full mission impact.

And this is the space in which pastors like Sutton Turner live and serve so that the church grows deeper and wider. And this is also the space that is often vacant among leadership teams in many churches. We need more pastors to serve churches in the manner Pastor Sutton Turner has served Mars Hill Church.

My prayer is that this book will be both compelling and helpful. I am asking Jesus to raise up an army of executive pastors to serve his church, whether they do so vocationally or as volunteers. And I'm hoping that many will make the same transition that Pastor Sutton has made. I pray that as you read this book, you too will take the invaluable lessons you have learned in the marketplace and apply them in love, in the church.

I also believe this book will be extremely helpful to those who are already serving in the executive role in the church. This book is way more than pragmatic; it is doctrinally practical. The Bible has much to say about how we do what we do. And there are good lessons to learn in this category.

This book is a must-read for lead pastors everywhere. As you read the pages ahead, you will have a far deeper appreciation and respect for the work of pastors who toil in areas other than preaching and teaching. And you will also learn how you, too, desperately need men like Sutton Turner in order to serve the church you long to see Jesus build.

Pastor Dave Bruskas, Teaching Pastor
MARS HILL CHURCH, SEATTLE

PART ONE

CRISIS

Trial, Error, and Jesus

CHAPTER ONE

SUCCESS FAILED

I STARTED DRINKING because I got everything I wanted in life. As it turned out, everything wasn't enough.

From childhood, I had set my sights on achieving goals, mostly related to all the stuff I wanted. I was a good little Texan, so of course my first priority was "to get me a ranch one day." By the time I entered business school in the late '90s, my bucket list had grown: I wanted a Mercedes. I wanted a big trailer and a crew cab dually to drive around in on my land. I wanted to be a real estate mogul, and I wanted to shuttle around in a private jet to see all of my properties. I wanted to travel the world. I wanted to do major presentations on Wall Street. I wanted to join an exclusive country club. I wanted a Rolex. I wanted nothing short of my own little kingdom over which to preside in perfect luxury and happiness.

Then a strange thing happened: all of my wildest dreams

started to come true. I enjoyed the luxury, but the happiness part of the plan didn't seem to be working. I had reached new heights of success only to see higher summits in the distance. Every time I reached a new height, I realized that beyond it rose something bigger, better, more expensive, more fulfilling.

Along the way I got married because, *Why not try that, too?* Marci cared about God. I didn't. So during our courtship I feigned interest, and my charade worked. We got married, had two beautiful girls, and I got back to tending my kingdom of luxury, comfort, and business. My wife would take our daughters to church on Sundays while I played golf.

I neglected my family to pursue other things, but I convinced myself that as soon as we had the ranch, the vacation home, and $1 million cash in the bank, I would turn my attention back to them. We got all of those things, and guess what? I turned to drinking instead. I was 36. I had already accomplished everything I had set out to do in life. But rather than feeling satisfied, I was miserable. From my mansion overlooking a scenic river valley where my cattle grazed, to the multimillion-dollar company I built from the ground up, I couldn't enjoy any of it. All I could see was more work, more disappointment, and more failure to meet my family's expectations. At least with alcohol, I could get a nice buzz and escape the crazy life I had created.

My business continued to grow, generating more money for hobbies—which became another means of escape. I picked up bow hunting, a sport all about putting trophies on the wall, so I liked that. A gazelle head mounted in my living room showed everyone that I was not only a good shot but also rich enough to gallivant on expeditions to exotic destinations. In 2005, I left home and spent $30,000 to go hunting in Africa, in search of meaning yet again. Little did I know, meaning would find me.

Let me ask you this: have you found what you're looking for?

Maybe you're like I was. My circumstances were rare for a man in his thirties, but perhaps you've enjoyed a taste of status, wealth, recognition, and achievement, which have created an insatiable craving for more. Happiness and fulfillment always seem just one more promotion, one more zero, one more investment, one more car, one more vacation away. You'll be content once you get the job, once you get the house, once you get the wife and kids, once the kids move out, once you retire, once you can get a drink.

Or maybe you're more like my friend, Fred Adams. Fred also carved out a successful career based in real estate and was semi-retired at a fairly young age. He was ready to do something else with his life and use his time, resources, and experience to serve and bless others. Unlike me, Fred wasn't looking for meaning. He had already found it, and eventually decided to give his life to the cause.

Or maybe you're like Adam Roberts, a young man I met recently. After a stint in the army, Adam has been getting established in his civilian career, presently as a logistics director for Dell. He's well on his way to financial success, but he feels drawn to the ministry. Since he doesn't have a seminary degree or any church experience, he's trying to figure out what it might look like to bring his skills into a ministry context.

While the circumstances of each scenario are different, the essential question remains the same: *How will you invest the rest of your life?*

Those of us from the business world often think in terms of the ROI ("return on investment"). Whether it's stocks, capital assets, technology, or whatever, we invest resources in order to gain some positive return or benefit. During the first half of my career, I paid great attention to my material investments but failed to wisely invest my talents, my skills, my experience, and my life itself. As I approached middle age, I began to realize that I was pouring all of these valuable resources into a bunch of junk that was destined for a landfill someday. Three decades of talents, gifts, and opportunities and all I had to show for it was a few pathetic toys and trophies, a failing marriage, and a drinking problem. Not a good ROI.

Having exhausted all of my strategies, I began to consider the big life questions that wouldn't go away.

What am I working for?

What am I living for?

What happens next?

This book is for anyone who has felt the same pangs of empty discontent, but it's especially for guys like me who feel a sense of urgency, perhaps even panic. Life will end someday, sooner than you think, and what will you have to show for it? I can tell you that not every midlife crisis has to come with a Harley and a divorce attorney. In fact, what feels like a crisis may actually be the Holy Spirit trying to get your attention. "Many are the plans in the mind of a man," the Bible says, "but it is the purpose of the Lord that will stand."[1] Somewhere in Africa, the plans in the mind of this man took a back seat, and I began to see the purpose of the Lord.

---

1 Prov. 19:21.

CHAPTER TWO

A KING, HIS KINGDOM, AND HIS MISSION

MARCI ALMOST LEFT ME. She decided to pray for me instead. I was not the man she thought she had married, but thankfully she believed Jesus could make me into the man God created me to be.

Before I left to play Rambo in Africa, Marci had one request. "Come with me to church," she asked. I fought. I didn't want to. I didn't need to. Three days before I left, I gave in and agreed to go to church with Marci and our girls. I wasn't going to like it, but I'd go. Sure enough, I hated it from the moment I walked through the doors of the Georgetown High School cafeteria. I didn't like the music. I didn't like seeing people raise their hands. I tried to make it obvious to anyone who might care that the only reason I showed up that morning was because of my wife. When the pastor took the stage, however, something began to stir in my heart. I was interested. Intrigued.

When I got back to the house, I jumped online and spent the day downloading two years' worth of sermons from the church's website. I loaded up my brand new iPod in preparation for my trip. Traveling 36 hours to South Africa and spending 14 hours a day for ten days straight holed up in a hunting blind gave me ample time to listen to them. Toward the end of the expedition, I heard a very powerful message about biblical manhood and leading your family, which ended with a call to respond. My hunting guide was there with me, and I'm sure he thought I was crazy when I got down on my knees right there in the blind.

I prayed to Jesus. I told him I was sorry. I asked for his forgiveness. I asked him to take hold of my life. I asked him to change me, because I didn't like the man I had become. I wanted to be like him. I wanted to serve him forever. Honestly, it was a simple prayer, but I meant every word. When I stepped off the airplane in Texas, Marci noticed immediately. "There's something different about you," she said. "Different" was an understatement.

I had thought that my business could bring me fulfillment. That my stuff could bring me comfort. That my hobbies could bring me happiness. That my money could bring me peace of mind. That my achievements could bring me validation. That I could create heaven on earth and rule over it as my own king. In the process, I had wrecked my health, my family, and my soul. Achieving all of my goals and expectations had only left me emptier than ever. I felt betrayed.

If you've ever chased after money, status, respect, power, or happiness and came up empty at the end, you're just like me and a million other men. The reason why it feels like it's not working is because it *doesn't*. You were not meant to build your own kingdom or be your own king or give your life to any other god besides the true God.

Before we go a step further, I want to invite you right now to stop. Stop running after stuff you can't catch, and turn around. Ask Jesus to forgive you. This is called repentance—and it's more than cleaning up your act or feeling sorry for what you've done. Repentance is a gift from God—a change of heart that results in a change of life. It requires an admission of guilt, that we are sinners in need of salvation, grace, and forgiveness—which God gives freely to anyone humble enough to ask. In this way, repentance is something we live out before God. But since our sin does not occur in isolation, repentance is also something we live out with our family, our friends, our church, and our community.

For me, this meant a number of changes. I met Jesus, and I realized that investing my life for his mission was so much more satisfying that squandering it on my own addictions, hobbies, and luxuries. With a new heart granted through repentance and faith, God also gave me new desires. I wanted to spend more time with my wife and kids. I wanted to take care of my body better. I wanted to pray and read my Bible. I started going to church as well—this time of my own free will. In fact, whenever the church was open, I was there. We had seven services at the time, so I was there a lot. I got baptized. I joined the prayer team. I introduced myself to the pastor. I actually started to enjoy spending time with God and his people.

You see, my wife's prayers and my midlife despair were fully met by the presence and power of the risen Jesus Christ. I didn't have the language for it at the time. But I was a "new creation."[1] There's no other way to describe such a dramatic transformation other than being born again.[2] Jesus took my heart of stone and gave me a heart of flesh.[3] He took my sin and gave me his righteousness.[4] He took my despair and gave me hope.[5] Jesus took the superficial identity

---

[1] 2 Cor. 5:17.
[2] John 3:3.
[3] Ezek. 36:26.
[4] 2 Cor. 5:21.
[5] 1 Pet. 1:3.

I had fashioned out of my possessions, wealth, and achievements, and he gave me a secure identity as a son of God.[6] Because his love is based on what he has done, not what I bring to the table, I could stop working, earning, building, and buying in vain. To make something of my life, all I had to do was receive Jesus' life. It's a free gift that God offers by his grace. And by his grace, I finally took him up on it.

The myth about grace is that it's a de-motivator ("Why not live it up if our sins are forgiven anyway?"[7]). In a sense, that's true. Once I met King Jesus, I was de-motivated to invest in my own kingdom because I realized it wasn't any better than a sandcastle. After years of trying earnestly to make a good life, my increasingly desperate efforts yielded diminishing results. But my ambition was reinvigorated by Jesus' presence. Rather than chasing the wind, it now felt like the breeze was on my back. I could finally do something truly meaningful in life because the source of true meaning had taken up residence in my heart. I wanted to know Jesus, follow Jesus, and serve Jesus—not to make him love me or bless me, but precisely because he already had.

I wanted to learn as much as possible because I was raring to go and make an impact for the kingdom! Although my heart was now in the right place, it took me a while to learn what making an impact for the kingdom actually meant.

Kingdom Work

Once you meet Jesus, or once you take Jesus' claim on your life seriously, some will say you need to become a "kingdom builder" and do "kingdom work." At least, that's the assumption made by guys like me. I had spent the first few decades of my life totally focused

---

[6] Gal. 4:7.
[7] Rom. 6:1–2.

on myself. After Jesus changed me, I wanted to do something more meaningful. I wanted to invest in the kingdom. But I didn't know what that looked like. Work for a non-profit? Start an orphanage? Get a seminary degree? Join the board of a parachurch ministry?

Looking for some answers, I read the book *Halftime* by Bob Buford. Mr. Buford wrote the book from his own life experience as a wildly successful businessman who walked away from his career during middle age, or "halftime," and started a number of non-profits that serve ministries and people. Likewise, he encourages others to take the capital they've accrued during life's first half (e.g., wealth, experience, networks) and repurpose their "time and energy into true second-half, kingdom-building work."[8] I really appreciate Bob's example. His story is incredible, and his work has been a blessing to me, to many others, and to many churches. But for Christians looking to make the transition "from success to significance" (i.e., *Halftime*'s subtitle), there's more to consider.

For one thing, there's much confusion surrounding the concept of "kingdom-building work." Search the Web and you'll find media companies, luxury homebuilders, church congregations, consulting firms, and countless faith-based endeavors dedicated to "building the kingdom." Did Jesus really have all of that in mind when he announced, "The kingdom of God has come near to you"?[9] Second, and probably more important, is building the kingdom actually what God wants us to do?

Kingdom Builder

The simple Sunday school definition of the "kingdom of God" is God's people living in God's place under God's rule.[10] This concept is

[8] Bob Buford, *Halftime: Changing Your Game Plan from Success to Significance* (Grand Rapids, MI: Zondervan, 1994), 74.
[9] Luke 10:9.
[10] David Helm, *God's Big Picture Story Bible* (Wheaton, IL: Crossway, 2001), 450.

arguably the mega theme of Scripture. The Old Testament includes numerous prophecies and allusions to a Messiah who will rule over God's kingdom, and the New Testament contains over sixty direct references to the "kingdom of God"—fifty in the Gospel accounts alone. Theologian Robert Capon says, "If Scripture has a single subject at all, it is the mystery of the kingdom of God."[11]

The first words of Jesus' earthly ministry were, "The time is fulfilled, and the kingdom of God is at hand; repent and believe in the gospel."[12] In the ancient world, "gospel" was a war term that meant "good news." A messenger brought word of an army's victory by proclaiming the "gospel" to a nation's people. Similarly, each time a sinner repents and believes the good news of Jesus' victory, God claims more territory from enemy forces, or Satan's kingdom,[13] and God's kingdom grows. This supernatural transaction is made possible by Jesus' sacrifice, and the good news is offered as a free gift of God's grace. We can't take any of the credit, any more than the citizen of an empire can take credit for a successful battle he only heard about. The victory is not ours to accomplish, but it is ours to enjoy. As theology professor Michael Horton puts it, "It is not a kingdom that we are *building*, but a kingdom that we are *receiving*."[14]

Collectively, the redeemed people of God's kingdom are known as the church. Jesus said, "I will build my church."[15] He is the kingdom builder, not us. That doesn't mean we can't do kingdom work. But it does mean that, in order for our efforts to be truly kingdom-oriented, we've got to follow the instructions of our King. There's nothing wrong with helping people, giving back, or working for a good cause. All for it. But non-Christians can do that stuff as well.

---

[11] Robert Farrar Capon, *Kingdom, Grace, Judgment: Paradox, Outrage, and Vindication in the Parables of Jesus* (Grand Rapids, MI: Eerdmans, 2002), 15.
[12] Mark 1:15.
[13] John 12:31.
[14] Michael Horton, "Renewing the Great Commission," accessed April 7, 2013, http://theresurgence.com/files/pdfs/ Horton_Renewing-the-Great-Commission-full-article.pdf.
[15] Matt. 16:18.

Many ministries have watered down the importance of sharing the Good News of Jesus Christ, preferring to "show people the gospel." But it is important to realize that people come to faith in Jesus by hearing the Word of God. You cannot see the death, burial, and resurrection of Jesus—you hear about it. When people hear the truth of Jesus, the Holy Spirit moves hearts to respond, and God adds one more to his kingdom.

Kingdom Citizens

As *the* kingdom builder, Jesus left his followers with specific instructions on how the work was to be done. His directions are known as the Great Commission:

> And Jesus came and said to them, "All authority in heaven and on earth has been given to me. Go therefore and make disciples of all nations, baptizing them in the name of the Father and of the Son and of the Holy Spirit, teaching them to observe all that I have commanded you. And behold, I am with you always, to the end of the age."[16]

Once again, Jesus establishes his role as the active agent in the kingdom. The only reason why we have any kingdom work to do in the first place is because King Jesus has "all authority in heaven and on earth" and is with us "to the end of the age." He has conquered, he is building, he is at work, he is with us—*therefore* we can do something truly meaningful for the kingdom: make disciples of all nations.

The means Jesus gives us to do so are baptism and teaching.

---

[16] Matt. 28:18–20.

Kingdom work begins with the proclamation of the gospel. People respond in repentance and faith, and kingdom work continues when we welcome them into the family of God (i.e., through baptism) and teach them what it looks like to live for Jesus. As new believers desire to share the gift of salvation with others, they start participating in kingdom work as well. The cycle continues: the kingdom grows and the result is the church, the gathered people of God. "It is to the church, not to parachurch ministries, that Christ has entrusted the Great Commission," Dr. Horton explains. "It is the church itself that comes into being through this ministry of Word and sacrament; it is the church that ministers these means of grace, and it is to the church that the Lord adds daily the number of those who are saved (Acts 2:47)."[17]

Faith-based nonprofits are important. Christian business endeavors are important. Aid organizations are important. But there are many "kingdom businesses" being started while churches shut down all over the country, particularly in major cities. As a result, there are less Christians today in the U.S. than there were ten years ago. In cities like Seattle, San Francisco, and Portland (Oregon), Christians comprise less than 8 percent of the population. Only one type of kingdom venture can possibly reverse that trend.

The church is God's chosen and biblically prescribed tool for reaching people with his message of salvation. And there's nothing that people need more.[18] It has outlasted nations, businesses, and the greatest of the great men and women. And it will outlast many more. The church is the only entity in all of human history that will remain into eternity, when the people of God gather in the place of God under the joyful rule of God, for good. Nothing is

---

[17] Horton, "Renewing the Great Commission."
[18] Eph. 3:10.

more significant than the church when it comes to kingdom work, though admittedly the church doesn't always look so impressive.

"The kingdom of heaven is like a grain of mustard seed," Jesus said.[19] Here's the thing about a mustard seed: it's not very big. In fact, it's tiny and easily overlooked. "The Kingdom of God which one day shall fill the earth is here among men but in a form which was never before expected," writes theologian George Ladd. "It is like an insignificant seed of mustard. This tiny thing *is*, however, God's Kingdom and is therefore not to be despised."[20] A mustard seed is small, but it contains all of the components of the formidable plant it is destined to be.

It's hard to get excited about a mustard seed, unless you realize what it actually contains. The world doesn't fully recognize the most important work the world will ever know. Political causes, social activism, and multimillion-dollar philanthropies will always attract more attention than the church, but the work of the church is more vital than any other effort—plain and simple. If you want to live a life of real significance, it's probably not going to look very significant. What most people mean by significance is glory—who gets the fame, the credit, the respect, and the honor. "I want to live a life of significance" can be a pious way of saying, "I want to be famous. I want people to remember me. I want to go down in history. I want glory. And in the process, maybe I'll do good things for people."

There's nothing wrong with a search for significance—God made us for a purpose. But ask yourself the hard questions: Who's at the center of your idea of significance? Am I really looking to magnify God's kingdom, or am I looking to build a monument to me? Real (eternal) significance seeks to make much of God—his

---

[19] Matt. 13:31.
[20] George Eldon Ladd, *The Gospel of the Kingdom: Scriptural Studies in the Kingdom of God* (Grand Rapids, MI: Eerdmans, 1959), 59.

priorities, his work, his kingdom. False (temporary) significance seeks to make much of me—my priorities, my work, my kingdom.

The life of Jesus demonstrates this tension perfectly. Nobody in the history of the world had the opportunity to make a bigger impact than Jesus. He said, "Do you think that I cannot appeal to my Father, and he will at once send me more than twelve legions of angels?"[21] Jesus could have made a much bigger splash than he did. But he knew that true significance was to be had in patient, humble faithfulness to the plans of God the Father. Ladd observes:

> [The] kingdom has come in One who is meek and
> lowly, who is destined to be put to death, who has only a
> handful of disciples. Little wonder the Roman historians
> hardly mention the career of Jesus. From the world's point
> of view, His person and mission could be ignored.[22]

I'm all for Christians achieving great success and establishing an enduring legacy during their life on earth, by God's grace. If that's your endgame, however, then the significance you're after is only fleeting, which means it's really not that significant after all. "But seek first the kingdom of God and his righteousness," Jesus said, "and all these things will be added to you."[23] In some cases, a life lived for the kingdom may look significant to the world, but usually it will look rather plain, perhaps even wasted. The irony of true significance—significance in God's eyes—is that we must be willing to live in obscurity in order to get it. Perhaps that's why Jesus said, "Whoever finds his life will lose it, and whoever loses his life for my sake will find it."[24] Like Jesus, are you prepared

[21] Matt. 26:53.
[22] Ladd, The Gospel of the Kingdom, 61.
[23] Matt. 6:33.
[24] Matt. 10:39.

to lead a life of significance, even if it means you will be largely ignored by the world and by posterity?

The church needs men and women of such courage. Each Christian may have a different calling, but our mission is the same. Very simply, we want more people to go to heaven and less people to go to hell. Only God can save a sinner, but he has entrusted to his people, *the church*, this life-and-death message of salvation. Every church, despite external differences, must be devoted to this single mission: Jesus' mission. It's all about more people meeting Jesus, more people getting saved by Jesus, and more people growing in Jesus. That's Jesus' mission, and he invites us to join. For some of us, however, it takes a while to get the message.

CHAPTER THREE

JESUS RUINED MY CAREER

Jesus was always speaking to me, but I didn't hear him until I started listening. His voice didn't resonate in the audible sense, but I could sense the Holy Spirit guiding my life, leading me in prayer, and revealing his wisdom through the Bible and through my pastor. I wanted to go where God wanted to lead me. And I would come to find out he had a pretty crazy trip in store.

Shortly after I returned from my experience in Africa, I reached out to my pastor. Joe Champion didn't know me for anything, but he was gracious enough to meet for breakfast. We struck up a friendship and started playing golf together. I look back now and realize my time as a new Christian hanging out with Pastor Joe was model discipleship: he didn't lecture me or take me through any curriculum; he simply became my friend. Over the next year, Jesus used this relationship to teach me, care for me, mature me, and sanctify me. I didn't know how long this season of personal mentoring would last, so I wanted to absorb as much as possible. Pastor Joe traveled the world for speaking gigs, and I had the means to tag along. I followed him to Calgary, Moscow, Paris, and Australia. He was teaching me the whole time, and I was just listening, praying, reading my Bible, and learning as much as I could about what it means to follow Jesus.

Back home in Austin, I got more and more involved in the life of our church. At one point, one of the pastors asked if I would take a look at the financial books. The church was growing like crazy, attendance was up into the thousands, and everything appeared healthy on the outside, but something didn't seem right. I reviewed the data and, to my absolute shock, discovered that the church was in significant trouble. The staff was huge and we only had sixty days of cash left. Operations were unsustainable, and it was only a matter of time before the church would fail to make payroll.

In the Bible, Pharaoh calls on Joseph to interpret his dream and Joseph has to deliver some bad news: seven years of plenty will be followed by seven years of famine. Likewise, I had to tell Pastor Joe that he would be up against a huge mess unless somebody made some changes very, very fast. In the Joseph story, upon hearing about the crisis at hand, Pharaoh surprises everyone by putting Joseph in charge of the kingdom. I felt equally shocked when Pastor Joe turned to me and said that I was the man for the job.

God's Family Could Use an MBA

The financial bind that threatened my church wasn't the result of any malicious activity or misappropriation. The guy in charge of operations simply didn't know how to run a business.

Now, I realize I must tread carefully. Ever since the first business guy turned out to be a crook—we'll talk more about Judas later, not to mention the many charlatans who have followed in his footsteps—church and business have endured a rocky relationship. So, let me be clear: The church is not a business; it's a family.[1] But a church does business because it's a family.[2] Every family must engage in business: we work a job in order to provide; we create a budget to make sure income stays ahead of expenses; we go to the store for groceries; we save for college; we do repairs around the house; we pay bills; we create various systems to coordinate schedules and juggle the responsibilities of life. The larger the family, the more complicated the business.

Most people don't see the need for business in the church because they don't see the church as a family. Rather, they see it as a Sunday school that needs a preacher, a care center that needs counselors, or a soup kitchen that needs social workers. Nobody really likes to talk about the business side of the family, even though churches are notoriously weak in this area. Some Christians treat business as if it were the devil's handiwork—like rock and roll, tattoos, or caffeine. Admittedly, these fears find substance in the many swindlers, cheats, and false teachers littered throughout church history. But the fact remains that many church families conduct complicated business—real estate, salary, programs, and more. Planting and leading a church in the developed world is more difficult than ever before; pastors face a dense web of red tape in the form of parking regulations, lease provisions, tax codes, health insurance laws, financing, ADA restrictions, and more. Life gets even trickier for larger churches with multiple employees, multimillion-dollar budgets, legal liabilities, and thousands of people to manage. A typical church in the United States generates revenue, leases buildings, purchases

---

[1] Eph. 2:19.
[2] 1 Tim. 3:4–5.

real estate, hires and fires employees, runs payroll, organizes programs, maintains a presence online, drafts contracts, and faces many of the same decisions and challenges that any other business might face—and then some. Whether you're inspired or offended by the notion of the church conducting business, at the end of the day somebody has to make sure there's money in the bank. All of this requires experience, skills, and administrative gifts that the typical pastor simply does not have. Without dedicated management, the church or the pastor—likely both—will suffer.

My friend Pastor Dave Bruskas was the lead pastor of a small church for many years. For a long time, he could not figure out why his church could never reach more than about 200 people. It would do really well up to a point, and then growth would cease. What he came to realize in retrospect was that it's nearly impossible to handle more than 150 personal relationships, a threshold known as Dunbar's Number. "In the same way that human beings can't breathe underwater or run the 100-meter dash in 2.5 seconds or see microwaves with the naked eye, most cannot maintain many more than 150 meaningful relationships," explains *Bloomberg Businessweek*. "[In] general, once a group grows larger than 150, its members begin to lose their sense of connection."[3]

In Pastor Dave's case, everyone in the congregation was directly connected to him, and when he maxed out so did the church. Between the relational demands, the responsibilities of running church operations, and the pressure to compose a sermon every week, Pastor Dave did not have the capacity to create the systems and structure necessary to organize the work and, more importantly, develop leaders to share the load. Many pastors of moderately sized churches get overwhelmed with the details of managing

---

[3] Drake Bennett, "The Dunbar Number, From the Guru of Social Networks," *Bloomberg Businessweek*, January 10, 2013, http://www.businessweek.com/articles/2013-01-10/the-dunbar-number-from-the-guru-of-social-networks#p1.

a church. Oftentimes what they need is someone to come along-side and help run the family business so they can focus on study, preaching, and shepherding the flock.

Overseers Lead the Church

Because we have a tendency to treat the church as an institution rather than as a family, we suppose that leaders in the church must have some sort of professional credentials, like formal ordination or a seminary degree. That's what I thought, anyway. When I first became a Christian and felt God leading me to serve my church more and more, I assumed Bible college would have to be a part of my upward spiritual mobility. (I ended up going to Harvard Business School instead.)

I'm convinced that there are at least three reasons why many business-minded individuals don't apply their abilities for the good of the church:

1. Nobody ever asks them to lead in the area of their gifting.
2. They buy into a false dichotomy that separates spiritual work from secular work, which leads to the belief that only "spiritual" roles, such as preaching and counseling, are suited for church.[4]
3. They assume formal theological training is a required qualification for leaders in the church.

Think about it. Do any of these three scenarios sound familiar? Has anyone ever told you your gifts are invaluable to the health of the church? Maybe you've written yourself off because you

---

[4] In fact, the Bible says, "Whatever you do, work heartily, as for the Lord and not for men" (Col. 3:23). And when it comes to abilities within the church, 1 Corinthians 12:5 says, "There are varieties of service, but the same Lord." The passage goes on to recognize "helping" and "administrating" as two specific ways God equips members of the family to serve (v. 28).

don't feel qualified or suited to help lead the church, but have you considered what the Bible has to say about that? Let's take a look.

The Bible clearly describes the qualifications one must meet in order to be a church overseer, and a seminary degree is nowhere on the list. First Timothy 3:1–7 begins, "If anyone aspires to the office of overseer, he desires a noble task." This is a worthwhile ambition, according to God. The passage continues in detail:

- Therefore an overseer must be above reproach
- The husband of one wife
- Sober-minded
- Self-controlled
- Respectable
- Hospitable
- Able to teach
- Not a drunkard
- Not violent but gentle
- Not quarrelsome
- Not a lover of money
- He must manage his own household well, with all dignity keeping his children submissive, for if someone does not know how to manage his own household, how will he care for God's church?
- He must not be a recent convert, or he may become puffed up with conceit and fall into the condemnation of the devil.
- Moreover, he must be well thought of by outsiders, so that he may not fall into disgrace, into a snare of the devil.

Did you see anything about how many verses you've memorized or what degrees you've earned? Exactly. "The list is primarily about men being good Christians," Pastor Mark Driscoll and Gerry Breshears write in their book, *Vintage Church*. The qualifications have little to do with what a man does at church, and everything to do with how he conducts himself "in his home with his family and in his world with his neighbors and coworkers."[5] What it comes down to is this: an overseer is a man who loves Jesus and lives his life in obedient, worshipful gratitude; who loves and leads his family; and who cares about the church enough to want to help. In other words, if you can affirm all of the criteria mentioned above—if you love Jesus, your family, and your church— you may very well be qualified to serve in leadership as an overseer. Simple as that.

Have I convinced you yet? But maybe there's more to it than that. Maybe you messed up your life somewhere along the way, like I did. Well, so did Paul, one of the most influential overseers in church history. He writes:

> I thank him who has given me strength, Christ Jesus our Lord, because he judged me faithful, appointing me to his service, though formerly I was a blasphemer, persecutor, and insolent opponent. But I received mercy because I had acted ignorantly in unbelief, and the grace of our Lord overflowed for me with the faith and love that are in Christ Jesus. The saying is trustworthy and deserving of full acceptance, that Christ Jesus came into the world to save sinners, of whom I am the foremost.[6]

Before Paul became a leader in the church and wrote half of the books in the New Testament, he hated Jesus and violently

---

[5] Mark Driscoll and Gerry Breshears, *Vintage Church: Timeless Truths and Timely Methods* (Wheaton, IL: Crossway, 2008), 70.
[6] 1 Tim. 1:12–15.

persecuted the first Christians. But then he himself actually met Jesus and was totally changed. Jesus gave him strength. Jesus made him faithful. Jesus appointed him as an overseer. Jesus gave him mercy in spite of himself. Jesus saved him. The same goes for all of us. Jesus determines whether someone is qualified to oversee his church.

The Bible is very helpful in providing practical guidelines, but these guidelines are not meant to be a means of achieving God's standard of approval. A passage like 1 Timothy 3:1–7 can easily transform into a legalistic checklist. But they're meant to help us rely on God's grace and recognize the Holy Spirit's work in the life of an overseer. His stamp of approval is much more important than whatever might (or might not) be on your résumé.

Prophets, Priests, and Kings

Jesus not only qualifies overseers in the church, but he provides the job description as well. Two key passages in Scripture offer specific guidance for overseers in the church.

The Apostle Peter writes to the overseers of the early church: "Shepherd the flock of God that is among you, exercising oversight, not under compulsion, but willingly, as God would have you; not for shameful gain, but eagerly; not domineering over those in your charge, but being examples to the flock."[7] Overseers serve the church out of joyful obedience to the Lord ("as God would have you") and love for his people ("the flock of God"). Overseers shouldn't be in it for the money ("shameful gain") or the power ("domineering").

In the book of Acts, the Apostle Paul addresses the overseers of the church at Ephesus:

---

7 1 Pet. 5:2–3.

Pay careful attention to yourselves and to all the flock, in which the Holy Spirit has made you overseers, to care for the church of God, which he obtained with his own blood. I know that after my departure fierce wolves will come in among you, not sparing the flock; and from among your own selves will arise men speaking twisted things, to draw away the disciples after them. . . . In all things I have shown you that by working hard in this way we must help the weak and remember the words of the Lord Jesus, how he himself said, "It is more blessed to give than to receive."[8]

The big idea is that Jesus is the good shepherd: he puts overseers in place to protect and care for his flock.[9] Overseers provide oversight, not because they're good at being in charge, but because they love the church. God promises great reward for those who fulfill this task faithfully: "And when the chief Shepherd appears, you will receive the unfading crown of glory."[10] Talk about significance!

The job description God provides to overseers is vague, and wonderfully so. It's clear that we're to "care for the church of God" and be "examples to the flock," but the Lord allows great flexibility when it comes to precise responsibilities. That's not to say, however, that the Bible doesn't provide helpful insight on the subject. The Old Testament describes three offices of human leadership: prophets, priests, and kings. Theologian Wayne Grudem describes the function of each: "The prophet spoke God's words to the people; the priest offered sacrifices, prayers, and praises to God on

---

8 Acts 20:28–30, 35.
9 John 10:11.
10 1 Pet. 5:4.

behalf of the people; and the king ruled over the people as God's representative."[11]

These three roles carry over into the New Testament with the ministry of Jesus. "As *prophet* [Jesus] reveals God to us and speaks God's words to us; as *priest* he both offers a sacrifice to God on our behalf and is himself the sacrifice that is offered; and as *king* he rules over the church and over the universe as well."[12] Some even see evidence of this triad within the Trinity. Theologian John Frame writes, "Generalizing, we gather that the Father is the supreme *authority* [prophet], the Son the *executive power* [king], and the Spirit the divine *presence* [priest] who dwells in and with God's people."[13]

Frame and others have suggested that a similar model is effective for organizing overseers of the church. This is not something that the Bible mandates, but I do believe there is great, practical wisdom to be gained from the triumvirate model of leadership. Jesus is the perfect chief prophet, high priest, and King of kings, and as image-bearers of God and disciples of Christ, each of us will reflect aspects of his character in different ways. He provides the church with men and women who can lead, and their specific abilities will usually tend toward prophet, priest, or king.

Of course, all leaders in the church must perform bits and pieces of each area, depending on the situation. If we revisit 1 Timothy 3, for example, overseers must be "able to teach" (like a prophet), "not violent but gentle" (like a priest), and "manage his own household" (like a king). In general, however, each leader will be stronger in a particular area, and a team of overseers in a

---

[11] Wayne Grudem, *Systematic Theology: An Introduction to Biblical Doctrine* (Grand Rapids, MI: Zondervan, 1995), 624.
[12] Ibid.
[13] John M. Frame, "A Primer on Perspectivalism," *Frame & Poythress* (blog), accessed December 31, 2012, http://www.frame-poythress.org/a-primer-on-perspectivalism/.

church is most effective when they complement one another in the roles of prophet, priest, and king to fulfill the Great Commission:

- To a prophet goes the work of proclaiming the news of the kingdom, so that more people can receive it and be baptized. He is the primary leader, the main Bible preacher, and the visionary. If a church has any paid employees, it's the prophet.
- To a priest goes the work of caring for the people of the kingdom, making disciples, and teaching the family of God how to enjoy new life in Jesus. The priest is a counselor, a midweek class teacher, or a small groups leader. A church typically has more than one priest, usually serving as unpaid volunteers.
- To a king goes the work of managing the kingdom, wisely stewarding the resources God has provided so that the church can grow until eventually the good news reaches all nations. The king administrates all or some of church business and operations. At a small church, the king is probably a volunteer, while a larger church might employ multiple staff to cover kingly functions.

Between prophets, priests, and kings serving in the overseer role, in which area do you think most churches come up short?

A church doesn't exist without someone preaching the Word of God. Indeed, the book of Acts shows that the church was born when Jesus' disciples started preaching. We've got prophets: they're called lead pastors, senior pastors, and vision pastors.

By definition, the church is a bunch of sinners who recognize their need for a Savior. When a large group of broken people gathers together, the counseling caseload and discipleship needs are obvious and rather urgent. We've got priests: they're called counseling pastors, discipleship pastors, and small group pastors.

Unfortunately, it's usually not until the church reaches a crisis point before anyone starts looking around for a king—like when the budget is shot, the staff is bloated, the new building needs a fundraiser, or the lead pastor is burning out. God has entrusted to his church the sacred work of his kingdom: the Great Commission. With the right help, we can make the most of the opportunities, the time, the money, and the people God has given us to accomplish what he has entrusted to us. The church needs more kings. At my church, we call them "executive pastors."

Executive Pastor

Before Pastor Joe asked me to come on staff and help the church through its financial woes, I had spent the better part of a year praying that God would show me what he wanted me to do, since my life now belonged to him. The time had arrived, and I knew what I had to do. But I knew it wouldn't be easy.

A few weeks earlier, Pastor Joe had preached a sermon on financial giving. He made the point that, in the Old Testament, God asked his people to give 10 percent. "It could have been worse," Pastor Joe said. "He could have asked them to give 90 and live on 10." In that moment, I turned and whispered to my wife, "That's exactly what God's fixing to do to us, and he's preparing our hearts now for what's to come." Money had been my god for so long, and Jesus knew I needed the encouragement of that sermon.

When Pastor Joe made his official offer, we sat down in his office and discussed compensation. "I know I can't pay you what you've been making," he said. "But this is the best we can do." Unbeknownst to him, the number was exactly 10 percent of what

I had made the year before. I laughed so hard that I had to convince Joe I wasn't offended but really encouraged by God's confirmation: I was to be an executive pastor.

Not everybody was excited by the career change, however. Several members of my extended family thought I was making a huge mistake. At the time, the property management company I founded was a big, profitable piece of cake. The business churned out plenty of money and afforded me about as much free time as I could want. I wasn't looking to completely upend the good life, but now I loved Jesus and he made ruins of the life I had known. He changed my heart, my priorities, my goals, and my direction. I wasn't sure if my departure from the corporate world would be permanent or just for a season, but I trusted him with the next step that I could see, and I followed him. I wasn't crazy; I was called.

CHAPTER FOUR

YOUR INVITATION

THIS BOOK IS an invitation for business professionals to invest in the church—not only with their money, but also with their time, energy, and experience.

Most of you won't quit your job and start working for a church like I did. Many churches can't afford to pay for an executive pastor anyway. Pastor Dave and his church of 200 couldn't have hired anyone, but a godly businessman could have volunteered 10 or 15 hours a week as the executive pastor and built systems and processes to help the church grow to 400, enough to hire a full-time executive pastor to help even more. The church needs men who are willing to walk away from their careers and work as paid executive pastors, and the church needs men who will keep working their day jobs and serve as volunteer executive pastors.

Either way, we need overseers in the church who can think like a king and use their talents to run the family business.

With your help, the preaching pastor can focus on preaching and more people can hear the good news of the kingdom of Jesus. With your help, the counseling pastor can focus on counseling and more people can mature as disciples of Jesus. With your help, the body of Christ can maximize its resources to the glory of God. And when the King of kings returns he can say, "Well done, good and faithful servant."[1]

Jesus' disciples once asked him when he'd be coming back. Whether or not they understood the depth of this question, in a moment of rare directness, Jesus gave them a detailed answer. He concluded with, "And this gospel of the kingdom will be proclaimed throughout the whole world as a testimony to all nations, and then the end will come."[2] This is an incredible statement. As George Ladd writes, "When is Christ coming again? When the Church has finished its task."[3]

When the church fulfills the Great Commission, Jesus will return. Do you realize that your strategic insight, business experience, and entrepreneurial drive could play an instrumental part in ushering the Second Coming of Christ? Goals don't get any bigger, hairier, or more audacious than that. Talk about a battle to win, a mountain to climb, a hill to die on! It's the mission to end all missions. It's the only investment that will pay dividends into eternity.

Maybe nobody has ever asked you. I'm asking you now.

Maybe you feel church is best left to the professional ministers. I'm telling you, church leadership requires more than preaching and counseling. The "professional ministers" desperately need

---

[1] Matt. 25:21.
[2] Matt. 24:14.
[3] Ladd, *The Gospel of the Kingdom*, 139.

your help if they're going to survive in ministry, let alone make any meaningful Great Commission progress.

Maybe you consider yourself unqualified because you don't have a theological background. If you can identify with 1 Timothy 3 in good conscience, then you have the Holy Spirit, which is everything you need.

Maybe you'd rather make hay now and wait until your fifties or sixties before you decide to do the executive pastor thing. I'm asking you to consider whether there's any better way to spend your heydays than to invest them for the kingdom.

I'm asking you to think about it. And God may be calling you. How do you know?

Ask the Holy Spirit

The easiest way to recognize a calling from God is to hear it from Jesus himself. It's pretty hard to hear Jesus, however, if you don't love him. If you love someone, you spend time with them, you talk to them, you listen to them, and you're much more likely to recognize their voice when you hear it. God speaks. Though his voice is always legible in the Bible, it's rarely ever audible. But Jesus has given us the Holy Spirit as a source of wisdom, power, and guidance.

In my first year as a Christian, my travels with Pastor Joe brought me to Australia for a huge conference—40,000 people gathering at the Olympic complex in Sydney. The event included literally hundreds of main sessions, breakout sessions, and ministry tracks. It was impossible to take in everything, so I was asking God which parts he wanted me to attend. At one point, I felt like he wanted me to go to a breakout seminar for worship leaders. This was odd, because I'm a million things before I'm a musician.

Not only that, but the session was a mile away. And it was raining. But I didn't care. I felt like I needed to be there, so I went.

I walked into the room and felt the Holy Spirit stirring in a way I'd never felt before. The speaker taught about serving Jesus and serving your lead pastor as a "2IC" (second-in-charge or second-in-command). The concept was totally new to me, but God made it very clear in that moment that this was my calling. I didn't know where, when, or how—I didn't even know whether it would be in a church, in a business, or in a non-profit—but I knew that I was called to be a 2IC. Again, this was odd. Up until that point, my job was president, partner, CEO—number one. I never answered to anyone. But I wanted to follow Jesus, and it seemed he was telling me to follow someone else as well.

I needed to pray about all of this. I did, and in the months that followed, various 2IC opportunities came up, but nothing felt quite right. Within a year, I was working as Pastor Joe's 2IC in the executive pastor role. But that's not the end of the story. I kept on praying, and after a season of dedicated service, I felt the Holy Spirit saying it was time to move on. Pastor Joe wouldn't accept my resignation, however, and since he was my pastor and I loved him and I trusted his authority, I stayed, though I did ask Jesus to speak to Pastor Joe about the whole thing.

Six months later, Pastor Joe sat me down and told me the Holy Spirit had led him to John 5:35, which describes John the Baptizer's ministry lasting "for a time" (NIV). Likewise, Joe believed my work at the church had been for a season, which was now coming to an end. We worked together to execute a smooth, healthy transition. The timing was further confirmed when God provided me with a great new job, which was not available when I had tried to resign six months premature. I went back to the business world for a few years, working for Muslim companies run by sheikhs in Qatar and

Abu Dhabi, of all places. (Don't worry, I'll get to more stories from that detour later on.)

Eventually, I felt led to apply for a job at a church again, this time at Mars Hill Church in Seattle. I landed a job as General Manager, but after a series of unexpected events I found myself in the 2IC position to Pastor Mark Driscoll. Now that I'm here, this is where I plan to finish out my career. The Holy Spirit spoke to me in Australia, led me around the world, and is now fulfilling his calling for my life. It's an incredible, exciting, and, yes, at times, fearful thing to ask the Holy Spirit, but I can tell you, he is known to respond.

Pray, fast, meditate on Scripture, repent of sin, journal, and sing. If you're married, do all of this with your spouse. Pull close to Jesus, focus on Jesus, and listen to what Jesus has to say through the voice and presence of the Holy Spirit. If you don't hear anything specific, that doesn't mean you're off the hook: he may simply want you to proceed with the written instructions he has already provided, and perhaps involve a few other trusted counselors in the process as well.

Seek Confirmation

Oftentimes, God will use the spiritual authorities and confidants he has placed in our life to provide us with direction. Meet with trusted leaders in your church—pastors, small group leaders, close friends. Ask for prayer. Ask for an honest assessment of your capacity and readiness for a calling to spiritual leadership. And then look for the open door. If the opportunity doesn't exist, then chances are you're not called—at least not yet. But if your heart is for Jesus, if the need is there, and if you're capable to meet it, a calling may be just that simple. It was for Preston Mitchell, who worked alongside Pastor Ed Young Jr. for over twenty years at Fellowship Church in Grapevine, Texas. "There was no major calling," Preston recalls. "I just wanted to help Ed."[4]

For those who are married, it is crucial to involve your wife and kids in this process because you can't be called as an individual. You have to be called together. A calling to ministry comes at a high cost, not only to the ministers but also to their families. My first year living in Seattle was really hard. Really hard. It was our fourth major move in five years. We'd lived in two states and three different countries. When we came to Seattle in 2011, we were totally new to the region and the church. No friends, no family. My oldest daughter, Grace, was 12 at the time. At one point, in the middle of the transition, she turned to me and said, "Dad, we knew it was going to be rough. But God called us here, so it's OK."

"Us," she had said! I was so encouraged and reassured. My calling as an executive pastor is more than my calling. It's our calling, as a family. My wife and I especially are in it together. A wife and kids don't qualify a man for ministry, but they can certainly disqualify him. If your family's not feeling the calling, if your family's not equipped for the calling, then you're probably not called. Be sure to talk it through and be honest with each other. Obviously, none of us can see what's coming. But families need to make the sacrifice, make the decision, and step into the unknown together, believing, trusting, and loving Jesus as a unit. The going will get tough, and if Jesus is not the glue holding everything together, your family will crumble, along with your ministry.

My friend David Chrzan felt a strong calling to be a pastor, but his marriage was suffering. The relationship reached a crisis point when his wife left and told him, "Either you give up the idea of

---

4 Preston Mitchell (Executive Search Consultant, Vanderbloemen Search Group), in discussion with the author, October 2012.

going into ministry, or I'm not coming back." David realized he didn't want to go into ministry without his family, so he gave up the dream and focused on rebuilding his marriage. The couple continued to argue about the church and ministry for the next six years, however, until David reached a point of desperation. He pleaded with God to either change his wife's heart or release him from the calling to ministry. "Within eight months, God did a miracle in my wife's life," David told me. "She became my biggest cheerleader to get back into ministry." It took another six years before David started working in full-time ministry, but today he serves as chief of staff for Pastor Rick Warren at Saddleback Church in California.[5]

Meet with your pastor. Ask for resources to help you explore your calling. Ask him, "Where do you see weaknesses in me and in my marriage? Where do I need to grow?" Talk with your family. Discuss your calling with your kids. Pray together and ask for their commitment to wait and hear from Jesus. Seek confirmation.

Check Your Heart

The Bible warns that some "will be judged with greater strictness"[6] when they stand before God to give an account for their lives.[7] This makes sense, since by definition the pastor's role is to shepherd the family of God, "keeping watch over [their] souls."[8] The well-being of God's flock is at stake. He wants shepherds who will put their lives on the line for them like Jesus, not hired hands who will abandon them when threats and hardships arise. "The good shepherd lays down his life for the sheep," Jesus said. "He who is a hired hand and not a shepherd, who does not own the sheep,

---

5 David Chrzan (Chief of Staff, Saddleback Church), in discussion with the author, October 2012.
6 James 3:1.
7 Rom. 14:12.
8 Heb. 13:17.

sees the wolf coming and leaves the sheep and flees, and the wolf snatches them and scatters them. He flees because he is a hired hand and cares nothing for the sheep."[9]

The hired hand tries to turn his calling into nothing more than a career opportunity, at the expense of the sheep.[10] A hired hand works for the church because he wants a paycheck. A shepherd serves the church with or without pay because he loves Jesus and his flock. Of course, earning a living is important and biblical, and church employees should receive reasonable compensation for their labor.[11] But there is a huge difference between punching a clock or checking off the "I volunteer" box, and shepherding the church. It's a matter of the heart: at the end of the day, are you in it for the people and God's glory, or are you in it for something else (e.g., money, status, appreciation)? If you're called to be an overseer, then the work is worshipful ministry. If you're not called, then the work is just a tiresome job. Here are a few more key differences between work as a job and work as ministry:

- If you want praise and recognition for what you do, it's a job. If no one else besides Jesus needs to commend your work, it's ministry.
- If you do the job as long as it does not cut into other things (such as hobbies, family activities, etc.), it's a job. If you are willing to make sacrifices in your personal schedule, it's ministry.
- If you compare your lot with others who have more free time, more money, and more possessions, it's a job. If you pray for others rather than compete with them, it's ministry.

9 John 10:11–13.
10 Pastor Mark Driscoll's "Dear Hireling" letter is a must-read for anyone weighing the call and the cost of working for the church: http://theresurgence.com/2012/06/18/dear-hireling.
11 1 Tim. 5:18.

- If it bothers you when the phone rings on evenings and weekends, it's a job. If you see random calls at odd hours as opportunities to serve with joy, it's ministry.
- If you want to quit because the work is too hard, the pressure is too great, or your performance is criticized, it's a job. If you stick it out—until Jesus clearly tells you that it's time to move on—it's ministry.
- If you use the church as a stepping-stone, a payday, or a gold star on your résumé, it's a job. If you're working for the church because you love Jesus and you want more people to meet him, get saved, and be transformed, then it's ministry.

Nobody's motives are 100 percent pure. We all have bad days when ministry feels like an obligation rather than a gift. If you're truly called to ministry, however, your deepest desire must be to love Jesus and his people—and when you fall short of that, you repent and course correct as the Holy Spirit continues to set your heart aright. The whole thing is one big learning experience.

For example, I wanted to help my church, but I didn't want to be a pastor. Though my new boss, Pastor Joe, kept introducing me as the "Executive Pastor," I made sure my business cards read "Executive Director." That title was much more pleasing to me. My impression of pastors was based on a composite of stereotypes, mostly negative. I thought pastors were preachers, counselors, and, to be frank, sissies. That wasn't me. I had never studied what the Bible says about the "noble task" of an overseer, and I certainly didn't know that the role of pastor was synonymous. As a new convert, I shouldn't have been a pastor anyway, but God has always been very gracious and patient with me. I had a lot to learn.

In a sense, however, my strong reaction to the "pastor" side of my job description was appropriate. I could handle the "executive" part, no problem. Compared with managing a multimillion-dollar business with hundreds of employees, running a church was easy. Anyone with a background in business leadership could fulfill the practical duties of an executive pastor without breaking a sweat. What makes the work extremely difficult, however, is the spiritual component. Without a sense of calling, an executive pastor cannot endure the struggle and sacrifice required.

Of course, this applies to all Christians on some level. Jesus warns us to count the cost before we follow him.[12] We're at war.[13]

Casualties and Costs

When we join the kingdom of God, we identity ourselves as active resistors of the rule of Satan, who "prowls around like a roaring lion, seeking someone to devour."[14] Any poor soul will do, but from the very beginning our enemy has concentrated the majority of his efforts on the people of the God whom he hates. Whether you work for a church or just volunteer, the more active you become in ministry, the more likely you are to face more opposition from the devil in the form of opposition, sickness, temptation, despair, and whatever else he can come up with.

Due to the nature of our work and the fact that we have an enemy, pastors will sacrifice and suffer. There are the expected occurrences—long hours, minimal pay, weekend obligations— and the unexpected ones—a friend betrays you, your child gets cancer, your house gets robbed. Obviously, we cannot explain all of the hows and whys of suffering, but we know that Satan wants us dead, disqualified, or both. If you declare war on him, you're

---

[12] Luke 14:25–33.
[13] 2 Tim. 2:3.
[14] 1 Pet. 5:8.

identifying yourself as a greater threat to his demonic grip on the world, and he's going to concentrate more firepower in your direction.

Drawing from numerous studies and surveys, the Francis A. Schaeffer Institute of Church Leadership Development produced a report in 2007 that confirms the unique spiritual dangers that await those who decide to become pastors:[15]

- 100 percent of pastors surveyed had a close associate or seminary friend who had left the ministry because of burnout, conflict in their church, or from a moral failure.
- 1,500 pastors leave the ministry each month due to these causes.
- 50 percent of pastors' marriages will end in divorce.
- 80 percent of pastors feel unqualified and discouraged in their role as pastor.
- 70 percent of pastors constantly fight depression.
- Almost 40 percent said they have had an extramarital affair since beginning their ministry.

Keep your armor handy.[16]

In addition to spiritual oppression, being a pastor takes up a lot of personal resources. My salary cut was one thing, but there are also opportunity costs that come with the territory. A volunteer executive pastor who gives ten or fifteen hours a week to the church has that much less time to spend at work, doing hobbies, or even just resting with family. Serving faithfully as a pastor may cost you in career advancement. In extreme cases, it may even cost you a job.

[15] Richard J. Krejcir, "Statistics on Pastors," *Into Thy Word* (blog), accessed on April 7, 2013, http://www.intothyword.org/apps/articles/?articleid=36562.
[16] Eph. 6:10–20.

Even for an executive pastor who isn't preaching on Sundays or counseling people during the week, there's no way to escape the messiness of ministry. Serving a church takes a lot of time and energy because we "bear one another's burdens."[17] When John Piper first became a pastor at Bethlehem Baptist, the church he would go on to serve for over the next thirty years, his father wrote him a letter. Bill Piper was also a pastor, and he wanted to ensure that his son was indeed called by God to take the difficult road ahead. "Now I want you to remember a few things about the pastorate," the elder Piper began,

A mountain of problems will be laid on your shoulders and at your doorstep. . . . Then there are a hundred administrative responsibilities as pastor. You're the generator and sometimes the janitor. The church will look to you for guidance in building programs, church growth, youth activities, outreach, extra services, etc. You'll be called upon to arbitrate all kinds of problems. At times you will feel the weight of the world on your shoulders. Many pastors have broken under the strain. If the Lord has called you, these things will not deter nor dismay you. But I wanted you to know the whole picture. As in all of our Lord's work there will be a thousand compensations. You'll see that people trust Christ as Savior and Lord. You'll see these grow in the knowledge of Christ and his Word. You'll witness saints enabled by your [ministry] to face all manner of tests. You'll see God at work in human lives, and there is no joy comparable to this.[18]

---

[17] Gal. 6:1–2.
[18] Justin Taylor, "30 Years Ago Today: How God Called John Piper to Become a Pastor," *Between Two Worlds* (blog), The Gospel Coalition, October 14, 2009, http://thegospelcoalition.org/blogs /justintaylor/2009/10/14/30-years-ago-today-how-god-called-john-piper-to-become-a-pastor/.

Why would anyone in their right mind risk the attack and the sacrifice that comes with being a pastor? A good shepherd lays down his life because he believes in the significance of God's kingdom; because Jesus laid down his life; and because he wants to serve like a dad in the family of God, taking responsibility for the congregation with a heart that reflects the heart of the Father. The life and work of a pastor is joyful and rewarding if you're called, and overwhelming and dangerous if you're not.

Noah. Abraham. Joseph (son of Jacob). Moses. Gideon. Isaiah. Jeremiah. Hosea. Joseph (Jesus' adoptive father). The disciples. Paul. Throughout Scripture, whenever God calls somebody to spiritual leadership, it requires a sacrifice of time, health, reputation, money, comfort, security, or all of the above. It's not something you do on a whim. It's not something you do because you think it will be an interesting or profitable career. You do it because it's something Jesus asks you to do. You do it because you love him.

Before You Freak Out

The stakes are high; the bar is high. Impossibly high. That's kind of the point. Jesus qualifies us, calls us, empowers us, forgives us, and works through us—often in spite of us. But that's not just a sobering reality; it's also a liberating truth. The more impossible the job, the more we realize how much we need Jesus, the more our results depend not on us but on him. Remember, this is Jesus' kingdom, Jesus' work, Jesus' resources. We're just stewards and overseers. Being called is not God's way of setting you up for failure in an impossible task. It's a comforting reminder that he's the one in control. The pressure to perform is off. We can simply give it our best effort and trust God to work everything out, "for it is God who works in you, both to will and to work for his good pleasure."[19]

Speaking from his experience as a former executive pastor, my friend David Branker describes what it's like to find solace and contentment in a clear calling when faced with a daunting task:

> When you realize the sovereign God has called you into a role, that for you becomes a sacred call. The sacredness isn't in 'what' you have been called into, but 'that' you have been called. Knowing that the sovereign God had placed this assignment before me was all the evidence I needed that he would help me navigate the highs and lows that come with it.[20]

It's also important to remember that serving in a specific role like executive pastor is rarely a lifetime commitment. God calls people for a season, which may last a couple of years or a couple of decades. My first tenure as an executive pastor lasted about two years before I returned for another stint in the corporate world. By God's grace, my time at Mars Hill Church will last much longer. The notion of a seasonal calling is especially true for unpaid leaders. For example, when a man volunteers as an overseer at Mars Hill Church, he signs up for a year, not for life. The commitment is mutually evaluated on an annual basis, and most men renew their term for some years running. However, we recognize that life changes rather quickly, and different seasons require different priorities. A calling may be for a lifetime, but more likely it's just for a season.

After all, we're only on this earth for a season. Jesus' work began

---

19 Phil. 2:13.
20 David Branker (Celebration Church Global Leader), in discussion with the author, December 2012.

long before we got here, and it will continue after we're gone. During the season of opportunity known as life, we must decide whether to invest ourselves in efforts that, like us, are here today and gone tomorrow, or to invest ourselves in the kingdom of God. You may never become an executive overseer, but all Christians everywhere live under a general calling to participate as members of the body of Christ, the church. Again, exactly how we participate may look different during different seasons of life, "but God has so composed the body," the Bible says, "that there may be no division in the body, but that the members may have the same care for one another."[21] You are called to play some part in God's grand story as it unfolds in the life of his people.

Unfortunately, many people may have a specific calling on their lives that is drowned out by the cacophony of idols that we're inclined to listen to instead—comfort, money, possessions, status, sex, and power. By nature, a calling is hard. So we rationalize our disobedience, or we flat out ignore the Holy Spirit. Not everybody is called to leave his job and go work for the church. Not everybody is called to serve as an executive pastor. Not everybody is called to be an overseer. That's OK. But we are all called to be on Jesus' mission and use our unique gifts for it, so surely God is calling you to do something. Ask the Holy Spirit to speak to you, and be ready to respond in courage and faith when he does.

"When I first came to Harvest Bible Chapel, I just started volunteering and making myself available in different ways," Fred Adams told me. "I did my part and just stepped through the doors that he opened." As a semiretired former executive, Fred had time and experience to give. "There was no voice from the Lord," he recalls, "but there was a definite stirring in my

---

[21] 1 Cor. 12:24–25.

heart."[22] For many, that's how the calling will come. Fred didn't wait around for a voice from heaven to tell him what to do. He wanted to do something, he knew he was supposed to do something, and so he started doing something. He simply availed himself to the needs of his church, humbly and without any strings attached. God kept opening doors, Fred kept faithfully walking through them, and the Holy Spirit has used him greatly to bless one of the most influential preaching ministries in the United States, serving as the executive business pastor at Harvest Bible Chapel in Chicago.

Be honest, be patient, be ready, and be proactive. Look for areas of need rather than ways to further your own agenda or build up your spiritual résumé. Keep moving, and Jesus will direct you to where he's calling you.

What's It Worth to You?

It all sounds pretty crazy, right? Leave a life of comfort, security, control, respectability, and ease, and follow a King you can't even see, for a kingdom that still looks as unimpressive as a seed, on a mission that probably won't be finished in your lifetime. Believe me, I know how it feels. To this day, I have friends and family who think I'm crazy to trust Jesus and work for a church. Hard days come, and sometimes I even doubt my own sanity.

Jesus knew it would be this way. He taught, "The kingdom of heaven is like treasure hidden in a field, which a man found and covered up. Then in his joy he goes and sells all that he has and buys that field."[23] I guarantee you people thought that man was crazy. Maybe his friends and family looked at the field and laughed. Maybe his business partner knew the field's market value

22 Fred Adams (Executive Business Pastor, Harvest Bible Chapel), in discussion with the author, September 2012.
23 Matt. 13:44.

and walked away from the deal. But the man knew the truth, and it was more valuable to him than anything else in the world.

That's my story. The parable that follows rings true for me as well: "Again, the kingdom of heaven is like a merchant in search of fine pearls, who, on finding one pearl of great value, went and sold all that he had and bought it."[24] I pray desperately for reconciliation with those whom I love, the people who wrote me off. But I don't miss anything about my old life. Jesus is better than all of it. He saved me, he changed me, and he gave me "an inheritance that is imperishable, undefiled, and unfading, kept in heaven."[25] And in an act of extreme kindness, he called me.

The church is the most resilient, lasting, and meaningful venture the world has ever known. Jesus died for the church. The Holy Spirit fuels the church with supernatural power. God adopted the church and gave us a mission. The work of the church is my Father's business, and there's nothing else in the world I'd rather do than give my life to the family enterprise. In most businesses, growth means more money. Not so with the church. Growth in the church means more people get to enjoy new life in Jesus today and eternal life in the kingdom of a loving God. The fact that I get to be a part of that is such a gift. Jesus doesn't need me to build his kingdom; he invited me to be a part of it. He could have chosen a million other guys to be an executive pastor, but he called me. I couldn't tell you why, but I wouldn't have it any other way.

The kingdom may cost you everything, but being about our Father's business is worth more than anything. Is he calling you?

---

[24] Matt. 13:45–46.
[25] 1 Pet. 1:4.

A PRAYER FROM THE AUTHOR

FATHER GOD, I pray for my brother. As he reads these pages, I pray that his love for you, your church, your people, and your leaders will grow. And as he continues to learn about the role of executive pastor, I pray that by the power of the Holy Spirit you will encourage him, protect him, and challenge him.

If you are calling him to invest his life as an executive pastor, please make the calling loud and clear. Prepare his heart for the calling. Strengthen him. Provide the people and resources to train him and prepare him for the role.

And if he is not called, help him to encourage other brothers who might aspire to it. If his highest and best use does not involve an official role in church leadership, open his eyes to where his kingly talents can be used in the church for your glory. Reveal to him opportunities to preach the gospel and make disciples in every area of his life, both professional and personal.

Thank you, Jesus, for what you have done. Thank you that you took on our sin and shame and died for our sin. Thank you, Jesus, that you fought our battle and defeated the enemy once and for all. Keep our eyes focused on you.

As we plant seeds of truth and proclaim the gospel, Holy Spirit, please remind us that you alone soften hearts and that we have all we need for life and holiness through your power.

God, I pray that you would use the remainder of this book to strengthen us to build your church and bring you glory.

In Jesus' name. Amen.

NOW WHAT?

The Life and Times of an Executive Pastor

LOVE THE LEAD PASTOR

THE BIG QUESTION to sum up Part One is, are you called to be an executive pastor? Only you can know if God is leading you in that direction. If he is or if he may be, then I want to help you in the remainder of this book. The big question I'll try to answer for you in part two is, what does an executive pastor do?

Each chapter of Part Two tackles one aspect of the role: serving the lead pastor (chapter five), managing the big picture (chapter six), stewarding church resources (chapter seven), and developing strategy for church growth (chapter eight). Exact executive pastor responsibilities will vary from church to church, but I've tried to keep things general enough to apply to most any context. Since the job title varies as well, let's make sure we've got our terminology straight. When I talk about the executive pastor, I'm referring to the second-in-charge (a.k.a. "2IC") function within the church, belonging to the leader or team of leaders working closest to the preaching pastor or lead pastor. Regardless of who holds senior authority in the church (in some churches, a board of directors or even the congregation can outvote the preacher), in the vast majority of cases the preaching pastor is the most prominent leader in the congregation, hence he is referred to as "lead pastor." The executive pastor (a.k.a. "XP") is the lead pastor's right-hand man.

Some lead pastors may have one 2IC; other churches may have a small team of two or three. Leadership Network consultants Mike Bonem and Richard Patterson call this function "leading from the second chair."[1] Former executive pastor Wes Kiel wrote a research paper titled "The Executive Pastor," in which he includes a number of helpful metaphors to illustrate the role. Respectively, Kiel compares the lead pastor and the executive pastor to the CEO and COO of a company; the captain and first mate of a ship; the owner and coach of a football team; the president and provost of a university; and the "dreamer" and the "schemer" in an entrepreneurial partnership.[2] The general sense is that one leader charts the course and sets the vision while another works behind the scenes to make it happen. In a ministry context, however, there is one important component that may not be present in these other relationships: love.

Twenty Years of Faithfulness

Preston Mitchell was an up-and-comer at a company called Texas Utilities in the mid-1980s. He had a lovely wife, a couple of

---

[1] Mike Bonem and Roger Patterson, *Leading from the Second Chair: Serving Your Church, Fulfilling Your Role, and Realizing Your Dreams* (San Francisco: Jossey-Bass, 2005).

[2] Wes Kiel, "The Executive Pastor" (sabbatical project), 20, accessed on April 7, 2013, http://www.xpastor.org/wp-content/uploads/2012/12/kiel_executive_pastor.pdf.

kids, and a good marketing job with a lot of potential. The Holy Spirit started to shake things when the Mitchells' home church decided to plant a new church across town, and Preston and his family joined the core group. After the mother church backed out, the small band of families who had already started gathering at the new location decided to go ahead and plant the church anyway. They needed to find a pastor, however, which is why they ended up hiring Ed Young Jr. and Fellowship Church began.

The Mitchells and the Youngs were close in age—much younger than the rest of the congregation—and both families had small kids, so everyone hit it off. For the next five years, Ed and Preston built a strong friendship. Preston continued to work in the corporate world but was very active in the church. He served on a team of five part-time volunteers who worked together to help get the church going. As early as 1992, Ed asked Preston to join staff as his 2IC, but it wasn't until 1995 that Preston agreed to make the jump. "I was happy at the corporate level," he recalls, "and the job was providing me with money and challenges, and that was awesome. But there didn't seem to be anything like being at the church with Ed. I just felt that I needed to offer up my service to Ed."[3]

When he finally stepped down from his role as executive pastor in 2011, Preston had served alongside Ed for over two decades. What started as a brand new church plant with thirty families had grown to a megachurch of over 20,000 people. When I spoke with Preston about the whole experience, one theme in particular came up again and again: "I just wanted to do whatever I could for Ed to make things happen," said Preston. Even as Ed's profile grew exponentially over the years, Preston

---

3 Mitchell, discussion.

kept the same philosophy: "I just told him that I would take over and do the stuff he didn't want to do."

Love for the lead pastor isn't about hero worship or hoisting someone up on a pedestal. It starts with a love for Jesus and his church, which results in an affection and respect for human leadership. Before ever meeting Ed, Preston and his family had joined a brand new church plant to reach a new part of the city. He had joined staff only after years of faithful service as a volunteer. He started working for the church not because he needed a job, but because he believed in the mission that much, and he wanted to do everything he could to help his lead pastor carry it out. Preston focused on implementation and management, and deferred to the vision, authority, and gifts of the lead pastor. This is very hard to do unless the lead pastor actually is your pastor: you trust him, care about him, and believe that God has called him to lead your church body.

Complete, Don't Compete

Lead pastors often have a tough time finding an executive pastor because they tend to look for a version of themselves: a charismatic gatherer of people who can help carry the teaching load. There's nothing wrong with having another preacher around as a backup or an apprentice, but the executive pastor role is different.

A lead pastor doesn't need a clone or a competitor nipping at his heels. He needs a coleader who can cover his weaknesses and watch his blind spots. The reason why there's no standard executive pastor job description is because every executive pastor must be a complementary match for the lead pastor. Wherever the lead pastor struggles—be it with fundraising, management, leadership development, guest services, or marketing—that's where the executive pastor must be strong.

If lead pastor and executive pastor share the exact same gifts (if they both want the pulpit, for example), they'll end up competing for preeminence, and the lead pastor may have a difficult time trusting and empowering a guy who could come after his job. Rather, the lead and executive should work like two pedals on a bike. A true executive pastor would never be in the running to replace the lead pastor because of their opposite skill sets. Rule of thumb: if the thought of getting on stage to preach the Sunday sermon makes you want to upchuck, you might be cut out for the role of executive pastor.

That's not to say that an executive pastor should never teach. In fact, as an overseer of the church, that's part of the role. But teaching a class on stewardship, leading staff Bible study, or presenting to the board of directors is a whole lot different than preaching every Sunday in front of the whole congregation. An executive pastor may teach, but generally he doesn't like it. And even if he does, nobody's going to prefer him to the usual guy.

In my present role, never in my wildest dreams have I ever thought about taking over for Mark Driscoll. He was born to preach, while for me any sort of public speaking is an act of raw self-discipline. I love working with finances, real estate, management, and systems, while Pastor Mark has never opened Excel. We need lots and lots of faithful preachers, and we need just about as many complementary overseers to come alongside these preachers so that the gospel of Jesus can go out more effectively and reach as many people as possible.

Do the Dirty Work

One of the easiest ways an executive can complement the lead pastor is by doing the things the lead pastor doesn't want to do. If you're an executive pastor, your job boils down to doing whatever your lead pastor can't, won't, or doesn't have time to do. If he's no good with numbers, your job is to manage the budget. If he doesn't like leading the staff, your job is to lead the staff. If he can't make it to every meeting because he needs time for sermon prep, then your job is to go to those meetings. Volunteer executive pastors probably won't have time to take everything extraneous off of the lead pastor's plate, so the first place to begin would be to help the lead pastor identify those priorities which need specialized attention.

More than any specific credentials an executive pastor might bring to the job, it's important that his passions and interests complement the lead pastor. Whatever is draining for your lead pastor must be enjoyable to you. A lead pastor's dirty work is an executive pastor's joy. Even if that's not 100 percent true all of the time, you love your lead pastor enough to take on the things he'd rather avoid, for the sake of the gospel. His highest and best use is your objective. When the lead pastor is effective and on target with his sermons and visionary leadership, the church thrives and the message of Jesus moves forward.

This "taking out the trash" mentality applies to other areas of the job as well. An executive pastor should be ready and willing to play the bad guy. A lead pastor wants to help people, and therefore he can have a difficult time saying no to requests. When I was working with Pastor Joe, we had an understanding: If somebody came to him with a request, he would either say "yes," or he would direct them to me. "Ask Pastor Sutton" was our code for "no." If somebody came up to me after talking to Pastor Joe, I knew that my job was to graciously decline whatever it was they were asking for. In this way, I helped guard my lead pastor's time and energy. The nos drain a lot more than the yeses. Likewise, if a church has a full-time executive pastor managing operations, he should generally be the one handling layoffs and terminations.

The purpose is not to shelter the lead pastor from reality or unpleasantness. In fact, withholding bad news from your lead pastor can lead to miscommunication and poor decisions that compromise the health of the church. If you only present rose-colored information, the lead pastor will fail to see the land mines until they explode. "No surprises" is a healthy rule for an executive pastor to abide by in communicating with his lead. The executive pastor is duty-bound to deliver the bad news along with the good so that the lead pastor can make informed, wise decisions based on the truth rather than an overly optimistic version of the truth.

Finally, when it comes to doing the dirty work, it's important to remember the difference between an executive *pastor* and an executive *assistant*. "I have to view myself as a leader to do my job," says Greg Hawkins, executive pastor at Willow Creek. "I'm not doing my job if I'm just an administrator."[4] An assistant helps the lead pastor *do more*; a second-in-charge overseer *does more* for the lead pastor. In my life as an executive pastor, I have felt like a glorified assistant from time to time. To a certain extent, that's OK. We must be humble and ready to serve in whatever capacity is most needed in the moment, whether the task is menial or complicated. But while an assistant accomplishes to-dos for a lead pastor, a 2IC allows the lead pastor to hand off major responsibili-

---

[4] Quoted in Bonem & Patterson, *Leading from the Second Chair*, 61.

ties entirely. An assistant mostly does work. A 2IC mostly leads others who do the work.

To a certain extent, it comes down to a matter of ownership and intentionality. Do you care about the church? Do you take responsibility for the work, even if you are doing it on someone else's behalf? "Don't look at yourself as number one's errand runner," Billy Hornsby advised in his book, *Success for the Second in Command.* "You may be implementing someone else's strategy, but treat it as your personal quest for success."[5]

His Vision Is Your Vision

Hornsby's words apply not only to daily tasks, but to vision as well. And like talent and skills, an executive pastor's vision must complement and not compete with the vision of the lead pastor. Bonem and Patterson put it well: "The senior pastor is sensing God's direction, painting the verbal pictures, and catalyzing the congregation, while the second chair is looking through the details of the facts, figures, personnel, finance, and ministry programs to ensure that the vision is actually being accomplished."[6]

The word "division" literally means having two different visions, which can be extremely destructive within a church.[7] An executive pastor cannot bring his own personal ministry agenda, priorities, or vision to the table. If he does his job well, he will garner great influence with the lead pastor and likely end up helping to shape the ministry, but this access is a responsibility to be stewarded rather than a perk to be exploited. The executive pastor must clearly see and fully champion the lead pastor's

---

[5] Bill Hornsby, *Success for the Second in Command: Leading from the Second Chariot* (Lake Mary, FL: Creation House, 2004), 61.
[6] Bonem and Patterson, *Leading from the Second Chair,* 146.
[7] See 1 Cor. 12:25; Titus 3:10.

vision as if it were his own. In addressing staff or talking with the congregation, the executive pastor's perspective should be, "This is where *we're* going" and not, "This is where the lead pastor says we're going."

One vision does not always mean there has to be perfect agreement between the lead and the executive. You're no good as a yes-man who doesn't have the courage or ability to raise concerns, identify red flags, or provide accountability. But where and how these conversations take place makes all the difference. "I've implemented a host of decisions I would never do myself," says long-time executive pastor David Fletcher. "But if the senior pastor and I made that decision . . . then it's my decision. You have the confidential discussions in the back room—disagree, fight, claw at each other, whatever you want to do—but when that door opens, it's one voice and one way of doing ministry."[8]

"When the time was appropriate, I would share ideas but never lobby for them," says David Branker, who also served as an executive pastor for many years. "Whether they were received or not received, it wasn't a burden for me to carry. My role was first a servant and a steward, not the primary decision maker."[9]

Of course, this is a whole lot easier if you love and trust the lead pastor, which means you must first know and understand his vision before you sign on. "The passion I had for the church was developed before I came on staff," said Harvest Bible Chapel's Fred Adams. "You should never become an executive pastor in hopes of changing the direction of the church. You should be excited about where the church is going."[10]

[8] David Fletcher (Founder, XPastor), in discussion with the author, October 2012.
[9] Branker, discussion.
[10] Adams, discussion.

On the other side of the spectrum, I met with one executive pastor who leveled all kinds of criticisms against his lead pastor. He would not stop griping about his church, and he blamed all of its problems on the lead pastor. He failed to win me over to his vision, and I finally had to stop him and suggest that he call his lead pastor for a rebuke. If an executive pastor cannot respect the vision and submit to the authority of his lead pastor, it's time to repent or resign. People change and the vision will evolve, so it's not a sin to disagree or even part ways. But an executive pastor can demonstrate love and respect for the lead pastor, even if they decide to no longer do ministry together.

An executive should join the pastoral team out of a desire to participate in the work God has already begun. If your heart is for Jesus' mission and his church, and you're the man Jesus has called to lead his sheep, then it won't be too hard to toe the line. "A first-chair leader is often like a master artist," explain Bonem and Patterson, "outlining a drawing and a color scheme and then letting a team of apprentices complete the painting. If the apprentices like the theme and the concept of the painting, they will enjoy completing the work of art."[11]

Stay Positive

If you love your lead pastor and own the vision, a positive attitude should come naturally. Then again, life is hard and ministry makes it harder, so you're bound to have some bad days. It's easy to justify a bad attitude by blaming our mood on our circumstances. But, interestingly enough, the Bible is rife with commands like "give thanks in all circumstances,"[12] "be glad

[11] Bonem and Patterson, *Leading from the Second Chair*, 143.
[12] 1 Thess. 5:18.

and rejoice,"[13] and "do all things without grumbling."[14] When struggling with a bad attitude, you can either (1) pout and disobey God, (2) feign happiness, or (3) repent and trust the Holy Spirit to change your heart.

We don't have the strength to fulfill all that the Bible commands, especially in the middle of all the stressors that come with ministry. God forgives us when we get cynical and encourages the joy we have in Jesus—so long as we choose to hear and follow his guidance by faith. By God's grace, we can repent of a bad attitude rather than remain enslaved to it. In Jesus, there is always hope and change for the better.

It is so important for an executive pastor to embrace this truth, not only for his own good but also for the benefit of the lead pastor. The lead pastor will struggle with all manner of discouragement, criticism, and obstacles. If the 2IC cannot be a source of encouragement and hope, it will be extremely difficult for the lead pastor to escape the pall of despair and loneliness that accumulates around those leading out in front. This doesn't have to be naive optimism served up with happy platitudes. A positive perspective focuses on purpose and opportunity, while a negative perspective dwells on problems and failure. Here's a comparison of the two outlooks:

Problem-focused people

- Are paralyzed by problems and fail to find solutions.
- Readily point out issues and criticize others.
- Focus on their weaknesses. They're unable to progress due to fear of failure.

[13] Phil. 2:18.
[14] Phil. 2:14.

- Resist change because they cannot see the benefit of a new direction, only the problems it brings.
- Never take responsibility for their actions but rather blame another person or problem.
- Don't respond to encouragement, don't want supervision, and don't listen to advice because they perceive themselves to be fully capable and self-sufficient.
- Are threatened by, rather than appreciate and learn from, others more capable than them.
- Enjoy mingling with other problem-focused people so that they can commiserate, criticize, and talk about problems.
- Fixate on the problems rather than come up with plans to overcome them.
- Bring their problems onto a team.
- Invent more problems because it gives them something to do—dwell on problems.

Purpose-focused people

- Never raise a problem without also suggesting multiple potential solutions.
- Approach challenges not as problems but as opportunities to shine and grow.
- Focus on their strengths. They know what they are good at and seek out opportunities to use their skills.
- Acknowledge their weaknesses and know the areas where they must improve.
- Respond to encouragement and correction because they appreciate feedback as an opportunity to improve.

- Remain upbeat and positive because they see the light at the end of the tunnel. Even in a crisis, they encourage others to press on and keep everything in perspective.
- Appreciate the abilities of others more capable, learning from them rather than viewing them as a threat.
- Want to learn and get better in everything they do.
- Are slow to take credit and quick to admit when they are wrong (and equally quick to correct the error).
- Focus on the success of the mission rather than on personal gain, status, or recognition. They want to see the objectives met and fulfill their role by achieving the end goal.
- Enjoy being surrounded by other purpose-focused people because they want to be a part of a strong team where everyone's unique strengths add value to the whole.

Quite simply, an executive pastor must be a friend, not a critic.

Be a Friend

The bond of friendship shared by a lead pastor and his 2IC looks less like golfing buddies and more like Jesus washing the feet of his disciples. It's a friendship with the added dynamics of sacrificial service, spiritual authority, and distinct callings. Before Preston Mitchell became the executive pastor for Ed Young Jr. the two men already shared great camaraderie because they spent a lot of time hanging out together and their families were close. "When I came on staff, I knew that our relationship would have to change," Preston recalls. "I knew that I could not be best friends with Ed and be working for him at the same time. It's hard for people to understand that dynamic. I knew that he would have to spread his wings, do other things, and be around other people, and that was OK."[15]

Perry Noble (lead) and Jason Wilson (executive) also demonstrate a healthy ministry relationship. Like Ed Young and Preston Mitchell, Perry and Jason have known each other since their church NewSpring first began and before Jason came on staff. "I respect him as the leader—24 hours a day, 7 days a week," says Jason. "We hang out with our families often, but I never approach our time together as if he weren't the leader anymore. This is a calling; this is not a job. It's not as if when we're away from the office, we're not called anymore."[16]

A formalization of the relationship doesn't mean two leaders can't enjoy a little levity and good times together. In fact, a genuine relationship is much better than a purely professional partnership. The professional aspect won't survive too long if the lead and the executive don't care for each other outside of job performance. And it really helps if a 2IC can bring laughter into a tough conversation, not make light of anything serious, but deflate tension and forge some bonds that will come in handy during tough times. Fred Adams says that his lead pastor James MacDonald describes himself as a "play baby" that is always looking for a chance to goof off. Because Fred says he's similar, they can "connect on some personal levels, which helps because ministry can be intense."

What this sort of interaction speaks to is the ability for the lead pastor to relax and let down his guard. If a 2IC can provide that level of trust and understanding, this is hugely helpful for the mental, spiritual, and emotional health of the lead pastor, which in turn blesses the whole church. In a friendship with

---

[15] Mitchell, discussion.
[16] Jason Wilson (Executive Pastor, NewSpring Church), in discussion with the author, October 2012.

his 2IC, the lead pastor doesn't have to be "on" all of the time and can unwind a bit by taking little breaks here and there to blow off steam, enjoy some laughs, and candidly process whatever is going on with life and ministry. Sometimes I'll travel with Pastor Mark for accountability, but since we also share a friendship, I can be a sounding board. A lead pastor needs a safe place to "dump his bucket." (Maybe that's a Texas phrase, I don't know.) The idea is that everybody needs a safe place to express their emotions. The first, best place to dump your bucket is in the presence of God, which is what the book of Psalms is all about. But it's helpful to have a human sounding board as well, when you're feeling really upset, angry, sad, concerned, or frustrated.

A lead pastor needs to be able to dump his bucket on the 2IC. Otherwise, he's likely to pour down on the congregation from the pulpit, which can be devastating for a church and harmful to the mission. A trustworthy and resilient executive pastor can absorb some heat in the context of a friendship without taking it personally. This allows the lead pastor to work through the raw emotions that might cloud his perspective. In order for this arrangement to work, however, the executive pastor also needs a place to dump his bucket so that he doesn't bottle it up and take it home with him. A trusted friend or another senior leader is ideal.

I realize that people may not like to think about their pastors venting or airing grievances. And I fully concede that dumping the bucket must never devolve into an excuse for gossip (i.e., rumors, slander, or disclosing gratuitous private details). But we often demand more grace from our leaders than we're willing to extend. Nobody is immune from the occasional bad day, the complexities of life, and the effects of sin. A lead pastor struggles with the same things that anyone else does. The only difference is that he must exercise much more discretion regarding what he says to whom and when. An executive pastor is in the ideal position to provide a place for the kind of honest conversation that is not best suited for general company. Also, if the lead pastor does not dump his bucket on the executive pastor, the executive pastor does not know where the pain points are. Even more than an opportunity to blow off steam, dumping the bucket can be a helpful exercise that forces to the surface real issues requiring further attention and discussion.

Watch His Back

Other than perhaps his wife, a 2IC knows better than anyone the struggles, pressures, and challenges that the lead pastor faces. This means that few are in a better position to pray for the lead pastor. And the executive pastor should be praying for his lead pastor every day. Don't just take the bucket dump: use those interactions to inform and guide your prayers for your friend.

An executive pastor is also in a unique position to ensure that the lead pastor is held accountable. Depending on the nature of the professional and personal relationship, it may not be healthy for the executive pastor to provide primary accountability (if the executive pastor is the lead pastor's direct report, for example). However, the executive can work with the lead to develop systems and policies that help him stay above reproach. This may be a simple thing like a code-of-conduct covenant that stipulates restrictions on access to things like the Internet and private hotel rooms. More complicated measures would include drafting sound bylaws and/or establishing an independent board to counsel the lead pastor on how to deal with charges that might arise.

Whether or not legitimate accusations ever come, criticism surely will. In fact, nobody in the church will receive more criticism than the lead pastor. As an executive pastor, you can't shield him from all of this (nor should you),[17] but you can and will take a few bullets by standing alongside him as a brother at arms. Mars Hill Church and Pastor Mark Driscoll face a lot of opposition—just ask Google. For some, this vitriol would be unbearable, but God used my time working in the Middle East to thicken my skin. Some of my colleagues hated me for no reason other than the fact that I was a Christian. Some would argue and contradict anything I'd say, even innocuous comments about the weather. What I came to understand was that this disdain was spiritual, not personal. That experience prepared me for the critics that we have against our faith. They don't hate us; they hate the Jesus in us. People are vulnerable, and Satan will use them to attack the work of God. Simple as that. Prepare to endure the thick of it so that your lead pastor doesn't have to bear the enemy's assaults alone.

This sense of solidarity, undergirded by the grace of God and the principles of Scripture, should inform whatever accountability policies you establish. Remember that the purpose is to love the lead pastor, not control or confine him. Objective safeguards allow him to operate with a clean conscience and a safety net, not to mention piece of mind for the church. Also, accountability may include advocacy on the lead pastor's behalf, making sure he is compensated fairly and treated with honor by whatever governing entity determines his salary, benefits, vacation time, and job description. If the lead pastor is a good shepherd, he will sacrifice even his life for his church. If the executive pastor is a

---

[17] Luke 6:22–23.

good 2IC, he will want to help carry this burden so that the lead pastor doesn't die prematurely but endures to the end.

Lighten His Load

All of this amounts to one basic concept: lighten the leader's load. An executive pastor can't make the lead pastor's life easier, per se, but he can help make it less complicated and more enjoyable. Know his schedule, know what stresses him out, know what encourages him, and tailor your interactions accordingly. For example, I have access to Pastor Mark's calendar so that I can vet opportunities, requests, and proposals based on how they will affect my lead pastor's world. I can also see when he is on vacation, out of the office, spending time with family, or preparing a sermon. I'll do everything I can to avoid disturbing him during those times.

On the flip side, when he is working, I'm working. No matter where he is speaking or meeting, I am physically present, if for no other reason than to show my support and help out as an extra set of hands and eyes. I need to see what he sees, do what he does, and hear what he hears so that he doesn't have to explain it to me later. By tailing Pastor Mark, I can usually anticipate issues and deal with problems before he even notices or brings them to my attention. As he makes comments here and there, I learn more about his preferences, stressors, priorities, and concerns, which helps me know what I need to do to lighten his load. If, for some reason, I can't be with him, I keep updated on what's going on, and I'm always available by phone. Also, I keep the pulse on what's going on within the organization so that I can (1) intercept potential burdens that would discourage Pastor Mark, and (2) spool up good news to provide him with encouragement. Again, the objective is not to sequester the lead pastor but simply to do everything within reason to relieve him of unnecessary burdens and distractions.

The lead pastor is most likely the most scrutinized, lonely, demanded, and vulnerable person in the church. An executive pastor who can provide some relief in the form of business and organizational knowledge can be of tremendous help. But even better is an executive pastor who can also provide the intangible benefits of a counselor, a sounding board, a burden lifter, and a friend.

CHAPTER SIX

FOCUS ON THE FLOCK

JASON WILSON HAS two photos in his office, where he works as the executive pastor of NewSpring Church in South Carolina. One is a canvas print of some of the 15,000 people who attended the church's ten-year anniversary service. The number "100,000" is written across the image as a reminder of NewSpring's vision to reach 100,000 people. Above this picture, however, is a photo of Mark and Mandy, a husband and wife who serve the church together.

Every day, Jason sees these two images representing the big-picture objective and the individual faces behind the goal. "I don't want my role to focus only on the 100,000 while it's somebody else's role to focus on the one," Jason says. "I want it to be both for all of us in ministry. When I get into a room to make decisions, however, I know that the decisions that the Lord has called me to make affect that big number, which is a weighty thing. I want my brain to think from that perspective, but I have to think about Mark and Mandy as I make those decisions."

The Bible compares the church to a family, which means every kid matters. But as any parent will tell you, a decision made for the good of the family does not always get unanimous agreement from every single kid. A dad makes hard decisions, not because he despises his children but because he loves his family. In much the same way, an executive pastor loves the church by overseeing the church and caring for its overall health. To borrow another metaphor from Scripture, an executive pastor has to be flock-focused, not sheep-focused. He must always keep the big picture in mind and make the greater good the top priority.

Focus on the Big Picture

A lead pastor needs a 2IC who can think high-level strategy and not wander off into the granular details of everyday ministry efforts. This is not to say that those details are not important, but an executive pastor must serve his function while the counseling pastor serves his function. "If the foot should say, 'Because I am not a hand, I do not belong to the body,' that would not make it any less a part of the body," writes the Apostle Paul. "As it is, there are many parts, yet one body."[1]

"I could have served by directing cars in the parking lot," says Fred Adams of his early days at Harvest Bible Chapel. "Praise God for everybody who serves in the parking lot, but for me it's not the same thing as serving in an area that I know well, like finances."[2] God has given the church and its leaders certain gifts,

[1] 1 Cor. 12:15, 20.
[2] Adams, discussion.

skills, and experiences. An executive does not pastor primarily by filling up his days with counseling appointments or service projects. This would be harmful and unloving to the rest of the church because it takes time and energy away from the areas where the executive pastor's gifts and abilities are desperately needed. An executive pastor must ensure that the organization is functioning in such a way that allows the flock to be protected, to be loved, and to grow. Here are a few examples of what this perspective looks like:

Sheep Focused	Flock Focused
On Sundays, you pay attention to just a few individuals. *Who needs prayer and counsel?*	On Sundays, you pay attention to the overall experience. *What barriers might discourage attenders and guests?*
Lead individual people.	Lead leaders of teams.
Make disciples.	Make disciple-making disciples.
Find a small group for a couple who is new to the church.	Build a database that makes it possible for many people to find a small group.
Meet the present needs of individuals.	Architect the long-term health of the body.
Tends to give ear to disgruntled church members.	Tends to have an eye toward progress.
Engage in individual interactions that lead to personal growth.	Engage in strategic interactions that lead to church-wide growth.
Maintain a weekly schedule.	Maintain a five-year plan.
Greet people at the front door.	Create a plan to close the proverbial back door.
Make decisions based on what's best for the individual.	Make decisions based on what's best for the whole church.

Obviously, the church needs leaders in both categories. Executives must prioritize the latter, not because it's more important but because it's our calling. It's what God has called and equipped us to do for the good of his body. Our senior pastor Jesus "gave the apostles, the prophets, the evangelists, the shepherds and teachers, to equip the saints for the work of ministry."[3] The overseers focus on the panoramic view, while the saints zoom in to make sure that everyone is cared for.

An executive pastor must be a pastor-executive who loves the group and the individuals. Executive shepherds must know the sheep, listen to the sheep, care about the sheep, serve the sheep, talk to the sheep, pray for the sheep, live life as one of the sheep, but always with the flock in mind. Jesus cares about each and all; we need to care about the many ones without neglecting our responsibility to the whole.

I want to point out that flock-focused leadership does not mean an executive overseer is not detail-oriented. In fact, he should probably be more attentive than anyone. Is the sanctuary too hot or too cold, and does it smell nice? Do we have background checks on file for all of the children's ministry volunteers? What events are going on locally that might affect the church's summer schedule? How can we fix the squeaky staircase that distracts the lead pastor while he's preaching? How much money is the church spending on business meals every month? All of these details have come across my desk as an executive pastor, and they all affect a large number of people.

Focus on the Mission

A church's mission is more than a corporate identity or mantra. If we don't do what Jesus has asked us to do, he has the

---

3 Eph. 4:11–12.

authority to shut down our congregation.[4] Therefore, we should take great care to make sure that the mission for our church is God's mission for our church. What does Jesus tell his people to do? In chapter two, we discussed how he gave us the Great Commission to make disciples of all nations, baptizing them in the name of the Father and of the Son and of the Holy Spirit, teaching them to observe all that he has commanded us.[5] And just before his final ascension, he reiterated, "You will be my witnesses in Jerusalem and in all Judea and Samaria, and to the end of the earth."[6]

Jesus made it pretty clear what we're supposed to do. He made it equally clear that our work depends on his authority and the Holy Spirit's power.[7] The Great Commission provides us with an objective, but within this broad framework, Jesus allows a great deal of freedom when it comes to methods, implementation, and exactly how we articulate the mission for our local church. Regardless of how you phrase it, communicating the mission is essential. People need to know why the work of the church matters. "A simple and clear mission statement is an important first step in congregational alignment," Pastor Larry Osborne writes. "It lets everyone know what you're trying to accomplish."[8]

Communicating the mission starts with the preacher. If the preacher is faithful to teach the Bible, the mission of the church will be grounded in the authority of God's Word rather than human ambition. In addition, "The values and principles taught from the pulpit eventually establish the DNA of a church," Osborne says. "Dropping core values and vision into

4 Rev. 2:5.
5 Matt. 28:19–20.
6 Acts 1:8.
7 Matt. 28:18; cf. Acts 1:8.
8 Larry Osborne, *Sticky Teams* (Grand Rapids, MI: Zondervan, 2010), 161.

every sermon makes them unavoidable."[9] The preaching pastor leads the way by establishing the mission, and the executive pastor affirms, reiterates, ingrains, and implements the mission throughout the flock. This is a "fundamental responsibility of leadership," according to management legend Peter Drucker, "to make sure that everybody knows the mission, understands it, lives it."[10]

At Mars Hill Church, our response to the Great Commission is to "make disciples and plant churches." "Making disciples" comes directly from the language of Matthew 28. "Planting churches" is how we expand this effort to "the end of the earth."[11] We want more people to know Jesus (i.e., become disciples), and join the family of God (i.e., church). In order to steer our vessel on the course God has set for us and avoid shipwreck on some alluring island of opportunity along the way, part of my job as an executive pastor is to keep the church on mission by saying "no" a lot. A clear mission is a very helpful tool, not only because it defines what you will do but also what you will not do.

"When I first came to The Chapel," recalls David Fletcher, who served as the church's executive pastor, "the church was spending $150,000 a year on staff for the kitchen. Within about ten months, we had let those staff go because their work didn't fit the vision of the church any longer. They were great staff, but the work they were doing was now antiquated." He advises all churches to "take a hard look at your vision statement—it could be a detailed statement or a general statement—and ask, 'Are we doing what we want to do?' Make the gracious but hard decisions."[12]

---

9 Osborne, *Sticky Teams*, 164.
10 Peter Drucker, *The Five Most Important Questions You Will Ever Ask About Your Organization* (San Francisco: Jossey-Bass, 2008), 13.
11 Acts 1:8.
12 Fletcher, discussion.

Focus on Priorities

A mission helps determine what you'll say "yes" to and what you'll say "no" to. In other words, it helps you prioritize. Assessing opportunities, making decisions, and setting priorities are all generally core responsibilities for executive overseers. Without a clear mission, you'll lack clear priorities. And without clear priorities, you'll have no way to filter the numerous opportunities, causes, needs, and ideas that surface every day. These opportunities may be worthy, all are probably tempting, but most are simply distractions. The church's mission should be the primary matrix for evaluating options and setting priorities. Here's how this generally plays out at Mars Hill:

Mission	Making Disciples	Planting Churches
Mission-critical tasks These top priorities are the areas of ministry that we deem absolutely essential for fulfilling our mission.	*Services* The church gathers weekly to hear the preaching of the Word, partake of Communion, baptize believers, and worship Jesus together as a family. This is the most important thing that we do, because through the church Jesus brings salvation and hope to the world. "Sunday is game day," as many of our churches like to say.	*Developing new Mars Hill churches* Though occasionally we send out church planters to plant autonomous churches, planting new Mars Hill churches has proven to be a fruitful method for reaching non-Christians.
	Community The church scatters for friendship, prayer, study, and mission. In order for a church to grow larger, it must continue to grow smaller. Community groups are the primary place where our people learn, grow, and receive care.	*Lead Pastor Residency program* In order to plant more churches, we need more men to lead these congregations. Our Lead Pastor Residency program provides a pipeline for developing effective, competent, and trusted leaders to take on new works.

Mission	Making Disciples	Planting Churches
	Training In order to help people grow as disciples of Jesus, we provide practical training courses, including biblical manhood, biblical womanhood, parenting, premarriage, and how to study the Bible.	*Real estate* In addition to a leader, new churches also need a place to meet. Finding affordable, strategic homes for our congregations is a huge component of planting churches and is therefore a top priority.
	Leadership development A four-week membership class and a one-year eldership track are just two ways that we "equip the saints for the work of ministry" (Eph. 4:12). More leaders can train more disciples, who can reach more people for Jesus.	
Mission-advantageous tasks These lesser priorities are useful for fulfilling our mission, but we cannot focus on them to the detriment of our top priorities.	*Business efforts (music and books)* Publishing books and music is a way that we maintain unity and consistency, and provide helpful disciple-making resources. This content also increases our influence, creating a larger platform that allows us to get the word of Jesus out even further.	*Mars Hill Global* While our primary focus is on the local church, we also want our "extended family," or brothers and sisters outside of our immediate church family, to benefit from our ministry. Therefore, we distribute free resources and provide support for church-planting around the world.
	Local ministry partnerships Obviously, the Great Commission is broader than any one church. Working with other churches and charitable organizations is a great way to get more done, bless the community in obedience to Scripture, and create inroads for the gospel.	*Mars Hill network* We affiliate with like-minded churches growing up in our wake so that we can help them be more effective and learn from our mistakes.

Mission	Making Disciples	Planting Churches
		Pastor Mark Driscoll events Strategic opportunities raise the profile of our lead pastor to provide a larger platform for preaching about Jesus.
Off-mission work This is where we separate our calling from the rest of the work we could do.	Cause-oriented ministries If we champion anything above Jesus and the church, it leads to burnout, distraction, or even division within the congregation. We organize food drives, and we encourage our members to participate in worthy causes, but we do not create or fund standing ministries that address a particular issue.	Parachurch support Though many parachurch ministries do good work, God's kingdom will advance through the church, which was established by Jesus and will be the only instituion that endures until his return—unlike any other organization, country, or ministry.

Sunday services are an explicit priority for NewSpring Church as well. "We want that experience on Sunday to be one that every-body in the community is inviting their friends to," explains Jason Wilson. A critical component of that experience is childcare, and they've developed a practical method for evaluating and guarding this priority. After Sunday school, volunteers will ask kids two questions: "What did you learn?" and "Did you have fun?"

"If we can answer those two questions positively, then we know we're gaining traction," says Jason.[13] "When somebody says they'd love to start a Monday night meeting at the church for moms to gather and pray for the kids, that's a good idea, but it's going to require a lot from the staff and it doesn't impact those two ques-tions for children's ministry on Sunday."[14] A clear objective with stated priorities helps leadership quickly identify ventures that might derail the church's God-given focus.

[13] Wilson, discussion.
[14] Ibid.

Oftentimes, however, this is easier said than done. Things get complicated when church members' agendas collide with the executive pastor's reality. I've had to fire staff, cut missionary support, kill programs, reduce budget, cancel events, and poke a baby seal in the eye (almost) in order to guard our priorities and stick to the calling that Jesus has given us. Some people get upset. Some even leave the church. But ultimately, we will have to answer to him, not a committee, a faction, or the flock, regarding how we spent the time, money, and creative energies that he entrusted to us for his kingdom.

A true second-in-charge makes the second most decisions for the church (only the lead pastor makes more). The more decisions you make, the more mistakes you'll make—no "mission matrix" or any other tool will change that. Jesus has called his overseers to make decisions, so proceed with courage, admit when you're wrong, and have faith that God's purpose will prevail even in our mistakes.

Focus on the Curve

My first stint as an executive pastor started out pretty rough. Right out of the gate, I had to lay off 40 percent of the staff. As I mentioned earlier, Pastor Joe Champion hired me because the church was in a tenuous financial state. We had to make some big adjustments fast or else we'd have run out of cash within a matter of months. All of this was unfolding behind the scenes. Everything looked totally healthy from the outside. In fact, we were growing by the hundreds! When news of the cutbacks reached the congregation, the church was embroiled in a state of frustration, confusion, and even anger.

Pitching the plane is better than crashing into the mountain, but extreme course corrections are never ideal. The necessity of drastic measures is usually a consequence of poor planning, inexperience, complacency, or a groundless optimism that assumes the status quo will continue uninterrupted. Failure to accept the inevitability of change lulls many churches into a sense of false security. You can't keep doing the same thing and expect different results. And actually, you can't keep doing the same thing and expect the same results. By the time a church realizes this reality, however, it's often too late.

The reality is, change marks all of life, beginning with our own personal journey from childhood to old age. A similar cycle follows every natural phenomenon and every mortal institution. In his book, *The Age of Paradox*, strategic thinker Charles Handy illustrates this occurrence with the "sigmoid curve" (fig. A):[15]

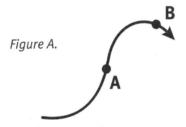

Figure A.

The sigmoid curve charts the course of inception, growth, peak, and decline. We can resist this process, but we cannot avoid it. Rather than deny or fight against change, it's better to learn how to get out ahead of it. Anticipate it, embrace it, and use it as an opportunity to thrive. An executive overseer will do his church and his lead pastor a tremendous service if he can lead it through the chaos of change and help everyone arrive safely on the other side. But how?

---

[15] Charles Handy, *The Age of Paradox* (Boston: Harvard Business School Press, 1994), 51–52.

Phase One: Everything Is Great!

When a church is on the up-and-up, everyone feels fantastic approaching point A on the curve. The congregation is growing, there are enough resources to care for everyone, and momentum is building. Nobody wants to make any adjustments because if it ain't broke, don't fix it. But this is exactly the point where an executive should begin to anticipate the other side of the curve and start taking steps toward rejuvenation.

When I first began working at both Celebration Church and Mars Hill Church, everything looked healthy from the outside. At the time, both churches were among the top ten fastest-growing in the nation, people were meeting Jesus, and small groups were booming. On the inside, however, financial strain and organizational disorder threatened long-term health. The average churchgoer could not see these issues, but the need for change became very clear to me as I dug into my role as executive pastor.

Phase Two: This Is Not Great!

The way to escape decline, Handy observes, is "to start a new sigmoid curve before the first one peters out (cf. Fig. B, next page). The right place to start that second curve is at point A where there is the time, as well as the resources and the energy, to get the new curve through its initial explorations and flounderings before the first curve begins to dip downward."[16] A new curve doesn't look so hot at first, not only because it starts with a dip but also because, if you time it right, it arrives when the first curve is still kicking butt. Change at this stage will often appear meddlesome, counterproductive, or even destructive. The change agent must champion

---
[16] Ibid., 51.

this effort with steel in his spine, because everyone will start to look for the villain who wrecked a good thing and the finger-pointing will commence. The old model goes head-to-head with the new model, which can cause a lot of tension and disagreement. "[The] shaded area is, therefore, a time of great confusion. Two or more groups of people and two sets of ideas are competing for the future."[17] Staff resign, people leave the church, and it looks like we took a wrong turn.

At Mars Hill Church, we had six months to chart a new course and steer clear of the mountain. At Celebration, we had 60 days. In both instances, the looming crisis related to cash flow. We needed to make significant changes in order to achieve sustainability. The changes were much more disruptive at Mars Hill Church because we had 129 staff and an annual budget of $15 million (at Celebration we had 28 staff and a budget of $3 million), plus 14 locations spread across four states. We centralized many of our operations to reduce inefficiencies and we introduced a new budget model based on weekly attendance rather than percentage of revenue (in other words, our various church locations would be allotted a budget based on how many adults attend rather than how much money they bring in, a more equitable and manageable strategy for a multisite church).

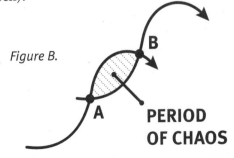

Figure B.

B

A

PERIOD OF CHAOS

---

[17] Ibid., 53.

Being the change agent is especially hard during phase two. Communication with leadership is crucial. All of the leaders must see the approaching crisis in order to understand the need for adjustments. Not everyone will see what's coming. Others may see it but then resist or resign when change hits too close to home and starts to affect their role, their ministry, or their staff. This is one of the toughest parts of leadership: when loving and serving the flock means making tough decisions that detrimentally affect some individuals.

Phase Three: Wow, Things Are Even Greater!

Eventually the second curve will mature, rise, and surpass the previous curve's high by God's grace.[18] Of course, this is not always the case. But thankfully, God can use failure to teach us, sanctify us, or prepare us for what's in store. When changes succeed, however, people will see the fruit of hard decisions, and everything will make much more sense in retrospect. Even so, "it is one of the paradoxes of success that the things and the ways which got you where you are are seldom those that keep you there."[19] In other words, the process must begin again and again.

After we avoided crisis at Mars Hill, we turned our attention to developing and changing things that were not in crisis but needed improvement. For example, we started rebuilding many of our key ministries: worship, students, kids, and women. We restructured our media and communications department. We created new leadership development tracks. And the list goes on. We're constantly looking for new opportunities and pushing in different areas, prayerfully looking for ways the Holy Spirit is calling us to stimulate ongoing growth.

---

[18] 1 Cor. 3:6.
[19] Handy, *The Age of Paradox*, 50.

Phase Four: Repeat

Every new curve is destined to follow the sigmoid pattern, and "the discipline of the second curve requires that you always assume that you are near the peak of the first curve, at point A, and should therefore be starting to prepare for the second"[20] and then the third, the fourth, and so on (i.e., Fig. C). Rather than a cycle of restless toil, however, "the discipline of the second curve keeps one skeptical, curious, and inventive."[21]

Once things settle down, people will want to avoid future change. The thinking goes, *We just survived all this change. Can't we just enjoy the fruit for a while?* Most leaders fall into this trap. Change can takes its toll on health and family, so the temptation will be to revert to old patterns after the crisis is averted. Such a response, however, will only invite the same mistakes and problems that led to crisis in the first place. A church or any organization will slip into decline when leadership stops thinking about ways to change things for the better.

Figure C.

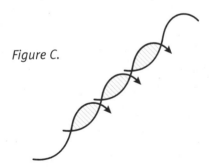

NewSpring Church grew to 12,000 people in just over ten years of existence. That's a lot of sigmoid curves. In the process, the church's leadership has learned a lot about how to shepherd

[20] Ibid., 57.
[21] Ibid., 58.

the flock through change. Setting expectations and frequent communication are essential to the process. "Our vision statement is: 'We're a church where change takes place,'" says Jason Wilson. "Obviously, the largest change we're looking for is people accepting Jesus into their lives, but change is consistent in many areas as we all grow. If you communicate that on a large scale, it becomes part of your culture and it makes the process so much easier."[22]

So what's the endgame? The upward cycle of curve upon curve can't continue forever. Bodies age, congregations decline, and nations rise and fall. Certainly, we cannot launch curve after curve in perpetuity. But we can use this model to transfer momentum to the next generation. This is not about the ongoing existence of one particular church but the future health of Jesus' church and the forward momentum of the gospel from one era to the next. Rather than riding out our own lifelong growth curve, at some point—before it's too late—we must allow the up-and-comers to launch the future from our peak so that Jesus' work might expand and resonate in our legacy.

This is more difficult than it sounds because it means letting go. And as Charles Handy states profoundly, "It is often easier to move on from disaster than from successes."[23] Preston Mitchell serves as a great example of what this transition might look like. After serving alongside Ed Young Jr. for two decades, it was time for a change. "I knew that I couldn't keep up the pace, nor did I want to, for the next 20 years. All of us as pastors and leaders have to look ahead and be honest about our lives."

Rather than mope into oblivion, however, Preston and his peers took the time to equip the next generation at Fellowship Church. "When it's time, you go gracefully," he says. "All of us

[22] Wilson, discussion.
[23] Handy, The Age of Paradox, 59.

have done a great job training the next generation of pastors. Ed feels as comfortable now as he did when we were there because we have a well trained staff. These guys are in a different season of the church, and I think we did a good job of finding these guys, training them, and being with them a long time before we left."[24]

As we call our flocks to set aside their preferences, their traditions, their familiarities, and their comfort in order to maintain a healthy trajectory, we must be prepared to do the same. In his research on growth curves, Charles Handy studied a family business operation that abandoned the textile industry for supermarkets at just the right time. He asked the matriarch where she found the courage to make such a drastic change. She replied, "We had the responsibility to provide a future for the family, and the past, distinguished though it was, could not have been that future."[25]

Likewise, may we let go of our torch while there's still time for our children's church to pick it up and keep running forward. In this way, guided by the Holy Spirit, the flock of God will never stop growing until Jesus returns.

---

[24] Mitchell, discussion.
[25] Handy, The Age of Paradox, 59.

CHAPTER SEVEN

STEWARD THE MONEY

"You've got the wrong guy." George Aghajanian's church needed to hire someone to help with the business side of things, and God led them to George. At the time, however, God hadn't told George yet. George had already carved out a career path, and it didn't include working for the church, despite the fact that he had made it his mission to give to the church from his substantial income. "One of my favorite Scriptures says, 'The wealth of the sinner is laid up for the just.'[1] Since getting saved, I've had a passion to tap into that 'wealth of the sinner' and bring it into the kingdom."[2]

George was good at making money, and he and his wife gave generously to the church. "My heart's desire is to provide for the

[1] Prov. 13:22, KJV.
[2] George Aghajanian (General Manager, Hillsong Church), in discussion with the author, March 2013.

93

kingdom of God, to provide for the church." He thought, *If I work for the church, I'm not going to be able to do that.* Despite his reservations, George agreed to pray about the offer. For a week, that prayer was, "God, say 'No.'" But eventually, George was convicted: "I didn't really want to hear God's voice. I wanted to hear my desires reflected in God's voice." He prayed some more. The Holy Spirit was persistent.

George's pastor was too. "Pastor Brian shared something with me that has never left me," George recalls. Aware of George's desire to provide for the church, the pastor said, "You'll be able to do more from inside the church than you'll ever be able to do from the outside." George didn't fully understand this truth at the time, but God convinced him to take the chance.

"The first thing I did when I came on was look for where we were leaking money, wasting money, losing money. No one does it intentionally, but the bigger the organization gets, the busier everyone gets, the less focus you have on some of the small things. But the Bible talks about being faithful in the small things," George points out. "Stewardship is about looking after every dollar, from the smallest gift to the biggest. It's the widow's mite."[3]

It didn't take long for George's focus to pay off. "I started to introduce some of the systems, renegotiated contracts, and eventually was able to save significant funds." In fact, George did exactly what God had laid on his heart to do: "I was able to provide far more resources than I could personally give."

When George started working for the church in the mid-1990s, Hillsong's weekly attendance was about 3,000 people. Today, the ministry has many locations in Australia that number 30,000 in weekend attendance, on top of the many more Hillsong locations around the globe in major cities like New York, London, Paris,

---

3 Mark 12:41–44.

Stockholm, and more. George has now served alongside Pastor Brian Houston for nearly two decades.

"The challenges haven't diminished. They've just gotten bigger," George says. "You have to keep looking at the inefficiencies, because the bigger you get, the bigger those inefficiencies could get if they're not addressed. We're constantly looking for where we're inefficient, where we're leaking money, and where we can do things better so that we can take that money and apply it to the ministry. No matter how big we get, that's a foundational truth that we have to keep looking at, making sure that the financial stewardship elements that we put into place many, many years ago can still sustain this rapidly growing operation."

When it comes to skill set, interests, and temperament, a businessman and an executive pastor share a lot of similarities. The difference is one works to make money while the other works to steward it. "When I was in the corporate world," George says, "it was about what I could get—the advancement, the promotion, the money, the car, being able to provide for the family—which is still important, absolutely. But now, that whole focus has changed totally." Now, George sees himself as the provider for a family of thousands. "As parents of the house, you provide the income, you provide the revenue, so that the family can live. We have to do the same thing: we have to manage what is in our hand to make sure that we can take the church forward."

Not every executive pastor at every church will oversee the finances. For many churches, however, resource management is a gaping hole, and few lead pastors have the time and experience to manage this aspect of the ministry. An experienced businessman could provide a lot of help when it comes to money. Ironically, however, it's oftentimes money that represents the greatest obstacle to businessmen stepping up. We're too busy chasing it to help the church take care of it. Churches struggle to steward their money while businessmen and other "kings" within the church struggle against the temptation to worship their money as lord and savior. I've certainly been there.

Idolatry of money looms large in our culture—any culture, for that matter. The love of money has destroyed many church leaders ever since Judas betrayed Jesus for thirty pieces of silver. People worship it, fear it, and generally don't quite know what to do with it. So before we talk about some specific ways that an executive pastor might help his church in financial matters, a biblical understanding of money is critical.

The Bible and Money

God has a lot to say about money. Thousands of verses throughout the Bible address money and possessions, and Jesus taught more on that subject than on anything else.[4] Obviously, a strong connection exists between our stuff and our soul. Much more can be and has been said on the subject, but the following themes provide a basic overview of what the Bible teaches about money.

Money—and Everything Else—Comes from God

The Bible frequently talks about the material things we have because all of it comes from God. "A person cannot receive even one thing unless it is given him from heaven."[5] This is why we talk about "stewardship." We're stewards—not owners—of all we possess, and someday the Lord will call for an account. Jesus tells a story to illustrate this point. A wealthy ruler departs and leaves three servants in charge of a portion of his assets. Upon

---

4 Randy Alcorn, *Managing God's Money: A Biblical Guide* (Tyndale: 2011), 5.
5 John 3:27.

returning, the ruler calls each servant to report on the "talents" entrusted to him. The first two servants took what their master gave them and doubled its value. "Well done, good and faithful servant," the ruler responds. "You have been faithful over a little; I will set you over much. Enter into the joy of your master."[6]

But then comes the third servant, and his report is far less bullish. "I was afraid, and I went and hid your talent in the ground. Here you have what is yours."[7] The master is furious. "You wicked and slothful servant! . . . You ought to have invested my money with the bankers, and at my coming I should have received what was my own with interest."[8] Our salvation depends on the grace God gives us, not the ROI we give him. But he gives us life, money, and resources for a purpose, not to hoard or to squander but to steward according to the principles of his kingdom.

Money Is for Using

As Jesus' story indicates, stewardship is proactive. True stewardship requires investing and spending, not just guarding and saving. In Luke's retelling of the same story, the departing ruler instructs his servants to "engage in business until I come."[9] This exhortation echoes some of God's first words to mankind.

After God creates Adam and Eve, he invites them to "be fruitful and multiply and fill the earth and subdue it, and have dominion over the fish of the sea and over the birds of the heavens and over every living thing that moves on the earth."[10] This command is known as the "cultural mandate." God gave us the earth and its resources as a gift, meant to be used and enjoyed rightly. Righteous

6 Matt. 25:21, 23.
7 Matt. 25:25.
8 Matt. 25:26–27.
9 Luke 19:13.
10 Gen. 1:28.

"dominion" over God's creation reflects God's perfect dominion over his entire kingdom.

Of course, dominion isn't always righteous. We're prone to take what God has given us and abuse it rather than steward it for best results and maximum benefit. Like fire or a gun, money is an implement that can be very useful or very dangerous, depending on how you wield it. Pastor and author Randy Alcorn says, "When we see money as a toy to play with instead of a tool to impact eternity, our vision becomes short-sighted and unfocused."[11] God gave his church a mission, and money is one of the resources he has entrusted to his people in order to accomplish the work. In order to be used for the mission, however, the money must travel from our wallets to the collection plate.

Money Is Valuable Insofar as It's Given Away

Money isn't *only* for giving away. The wisest man who ever lived (besides Jesus) said, "Moreover, when God gives someone wealth and possessions, and the ability to enjoy them . . . this is a gift of God."[12] It's not a sin to spend money in order to take a vacation, buy a car, or throw a fun party. The operative principle here is whatever you spend and whatever you save will be gone in the end, but whatever you give will await you in heaven. Randy Alcorn quips, "You can't take it with you, but you can send it on ahead." Jesus unabashedly promises eternal rewards for those who "lay up treasures in heaven."[13]

We "lay up" treasures according to what we do with our money. "For where your treasure is, there your heart will be also."[14] If you spend a lot on yourself, your heart is for yourself. If you save a

---

11 Randy Alcorn, *Managing God's Money*, xiv.
12 Eccles. 5:19, NIV.
13 Matt. 6:20.
14 Matt. 6:21.

lot for the future, your heart is for security and peace of mind in this life. If you give a lot to Jesus and his church, your heart is for eternity. Jesus told another story to his followers that drives this point home:

> The land of a rich man produced plentifully, and he thought to himself, "What shall I do, for I have nowhere to store my crops?" And he said, "I will do this: I will tear down my barns and build larger ones, and there I will store all my grain and my goods. And I will say to my soul, 'Soul, you have ample goods laid up for many years; relax, eat, drink, be merry.'" But God said to him, "Fool! This night your soul is required of you, and the things you have prepared, whose will they be?" So is the one who lays up treasure for himself and is not rich toward God.[15]

Like the fool in this story, it is quite possible to be rich in this temporary life and impoverished for all eternity. In the book of Revelation, Jesus admonishes one community of wealthy believers, "For you say, I am rich, I have prospered, and I need nothing, not realizing that you are wretched, pitiable, poor, blind, and naked."[16] You're treasure is only worth something if it's stored in the right place—"in heaven, where neither moth nor rust destroys and where thieves do not break in and steal."[17] In the act of giving, "The point is this: whoever sows sparingly will also reap sparingly, and whoever sows bountifully will also reap bountifully."[18]

---

[15] Luke 12:16–21.
[16] Rev. 3:17.
[17] Matt. 6:20.
[18] 2 Cor. 9:6.

Money Is Not Evil

At this point in the chapter, I imagine the Holy Spirit may be convicting some of you. That's not a bad thing. But what I do want to avoid is guilt. The easiest way to convince people to pony up cash is by making them feel bad. Tug at the heartstrings. Shame them for buying a latte every day while so many of our Christian brother and sisters go hungry. Such tactics may be very effective for the bottom line, but they're not at all biblical.

Poverty theology teaches that you're not really a Christian unless you give away all of your money and live on the edge of poverty, as if Jesus' words to the rich young ruler were meant to apply to everyone: "Sell all that you have and give to the poor."[19] Poverty theology is not compatible with the true gospel, because it's based on something other than the grace of God in Jesus Christ. Our salvation does not depend on how much or how little we have in our bank accounts. What matters is that our sin is covered by the blood of Christ.

From the very beginning, Jesus' followers came from very different socioeconomic backgrounds. The early church included poor people like Onesimus[20] and the Macedonians,[21] and it included rich people like Joseph of Arimathea,[22] Priscilla and Aquila,[23] and Lydia.[24] It's not a sin to work a well-paying job. It's not a sin to live in a nice neighborhood. It's not a sin to prepare for the future by investing in retirement. There's no need to avoid money or feel guilty about having it. We can worship money by idolizing it, but we can also worship money by fearing

[19] Mark 10:21.
[20] Philem. 1:10.
[21] 2 Cor. 8:1–2.
[22] Matt. 27:57.
[23] Acts 18:2–3.
[24] Acts 16:14.

it. God doesn't need our money, and it makes less difference to him if we're rich or poor. Ultimately, he wants our hearts, not our wallets, but the two are often inextricably intertwined.

Money Is Not God

First Timothy 6:10 is one of the most commonly misquoted verses in all of Scripture. Contrary to popular belief, money is *not* the root of all evil. The passage is nonetheless sobering: "For the love of money is a root of all kinds of evils. It is through this craving that some have wandered away from the faith and pierced themselves with many pangs." Jesus said that the most important command in the whole Bible is, "You shall love the Lord your God with all your heart and with all your soul and with all your mind."[25] When we chase after money, when we fail to give our money, when we find security in money, when money becomes the primary factor in our decision-making, then money has become our god instead of the Lord our God.

This brand of idolatry has made its way into the church in the form of prosperity theology, which reduces the God of the Bible down to simply a means for us to get to our real god— money. Prosperity theology encourages people to give money in order to get money back, and teaches that God blesses those who are faithful with material wealth. This destructive mindset turns Christianity into a get-rich-quick scheme, based on the misuse of verses like Malachi 3:10 (NLT), which says, "Bring all the tithes into the storehouse so there will be enough food in my Temple. If you do,' says the Lord of Heaven's Armies, 'I will open the windows of heaven for you. I will pour out a blessing so great you won't have enough room to take it in! Try it! Put me to the test!"

Charlatans use prosperity theology to bilk millions of dollars

---
[25] Matt. 22:37.

from naive believers who write checks expecting God to reward them with a miraculous windfall in return. Prosperity theology is an effort to shove a bit and bridle into God's mouth and hand us the reins. But we cannot control God, we cannot manipulate God, we cannot put God in our debt, we cannot give expecting favors in return, because he is God. And we are not.

God is faithful to fulfill all of his promises, but that doesn't mean his provision will always have dollars signs attached, nor will it always come to fruition in the here-and-now sense. What's certain, however, is that God has already given us more than we deserve and everything we need in Jesus. There is nothing we can do to put him in our debt because he has already paid ours to an infinitely gracious degree.

Money Is for Worship

Giving to the church out of guilt is poverty theology. Not good. Giving to the church in order to get something in return is prosperity theology. Also not good. Giving to the church in response to the work God has done in your heart is worship. That's what we want to see in our own lives and in the lives of our churches.

Before I met Jesus, I was a devoted worshiper of money. I wasn't a steward; I was the owner. I was going to get as much of it as I could and then do with it what I darn well pleased. There was no way I could even begin to "love the Lord your God with all your heart and with all your soul and with all your mind."[26] But when Jesus gave me a new heart and restored my soul and renewed my mind, I started giving as an act of worship. I realized that God gave me his Son.[27] I wanted to demonstrate my

---

[26] Ibid.
[27] John 3:16.

gratitude, reflect his generous character, and contribute to the work of the church so that more people could hear the message of new life that I now enjoyed.[28]

Martin Luther said, "There are three conversions necessary in the Christian life: the conversion of the heart, the mind, and the purse."[29] The act of giving requires dependence on God. We let go of our resources because we trust that God is good, and he will provide what we need.[30] Giving is a tangible way to place our hope in Jesus rather than in our own self-sufficiency. We may talk a big game when it comes to following Jesus, but our cash will flow in the direction of our true god. The reason God cares about our money is not because he depends on our contribution to the collection. He cares because what we do with our wallet reveals the allegiance of our heart.

That's why Jesus cares more about the proportion of our sacrifice than the size of our gift. The Bible records a situation in which Jesus saw a poor woman contribute two copper coins, the equivalent of a penny, to the offering. "Truly, I say to you," he said, "this poor widow has put in more than all those who are contributing to the offering box. For they all contributed out of their abundance, but she out of her poverty has put in everything she had, all she had to live on."[31] Our money and what we do with it is a spiritual diagnostic.

In his letter to the Corinthians, Paul instructs that giving to the church should be generous,[32] regular,[33] sacrificial,[34] and cheerful.[35] What may sound like a command, however, is actually an invitation. As Pastor Andy Stanley tells his congregation,

[28] 2 Cor. 9:12.
[29] Quoted in Alcorn, *Managing God's Money*, xiv.
[30] Matt. 6:25.
[31] Mark 12:43–44.
[32] 2 Cor. 9:11.
[33] 2 Cor. 9:6.
[34] 2 Cor. 8:3.
[35] 2 Cor. 9:7.

"Generosity is something we want *for* you, not *from* you."[36] God calls us to give, which liberates us from the grip of a lesser god and directs our attention toward the true God. We think we're in control of our money—where it comes from, where it goes, what we're going to do with it—but as long as we hang on to it and let it drive our life, the money is controlling us. "No servant can serve two masters," Jesus said, "for either he will hate the one and love the other, or he will be devoted to the one and despise the other. You cannot serve God and money."[37] We all worship something. If it's not Jesus, then it's probably money. Believe me, Jesus is a much better God.

The Steward-In-Chief

Depending on background, experience, and the needs of the church, an executive pastor may not work directly with money. Stewardship is about more than just money, however. The 2IC of any organization will oversee a fair amount of resources, whether that's money, staff, real estate, or other operations. The 2IC of a church is "steward-in-chief," keeping tabs on the details so that the senior leader can maintain high-level perspective. Here are some ways that an executive pastor may fulfill the stewardship aspect of the role.

Oversee Business Operations

The most practical place where an executive pastor can step up and lead is in the business functions of the organization. At the very least, most every church has a property to deal with, which means leases, contracts, maintenance, permits, parking, and all the

---

36 Chris Willard and Jim Sheppard, *Contagious Generosity: Creating a Culture of Giving in Your Church* (Grand Rapids, MI: Zondervan), 67.
37 Luke 16:13; cf. Matt. 6:24.

joys of real estate. Complexity increases as churches grow, adding gear, websites, vendors, legal bylaws, staff, intellectual property, benefits packages, and other components. Very few people with a ministry background have much experience dealing with work that is more corporate in nature, so any wisdom, help, or backup you can bring to the table takes a huge load off and sets the church up well for the future.

Unfortunately, many church leaders underestimate their need for operational help. "Most ministries want to put on a worship pastor or another senior pastoral position before they'll think of any admin roles," says Hillsong's George Aghajanian. "That's the wrong thinking. Although we're not up on the platform and up front, we provide a foundational basis on which the church operates."[38] This also means that, if you can handle business and want to serve your church in that capacity, you may have to be proactive. Get involved and look for opportunities to add value. Help the other pastoral leaders see what they're missing and how your skills could be used to better the church.

Set an Example

You cannot lead the church anywhere that you yourself are unwilling to go. Do you give financially to the church? Unfortunately, it's all too easy for church leaders to justify a lack of giving. After all, we give so much of our time and energy, and then there's the opportunity cost to consider—the list of excuses goes on, but none of them hold water. Chris Willard and Jim Sheppard compiled years of research and observations on church giving for their book, *Contagious Generosity*, and explain "Generous churches are led by generous pastors. Period." It's

[38] Aghajanian, discussion.

possible to be a generous pastor of an ungenerous church. But we have never seen a generous church that is not led by a generous pastor.[39]

It's important to know whether or not church staff, elders, and/ or key leaders are giving generously—not to coerce or intimidate anyone but rather to gauge the heart of your church. Your leaders should care more than anyone else about the well-being of the church. If their money is not in it, then their hearts aren't in it either. And if your staff hardly cares, I guarantee you that your congregation doesn't care either, which means the problem is deeper than lack of giving. At Mars Hill, before we ever talk money to the church, we check the giving of our elders and staff in order to avoid hypocrisy in our message and in our midst. Like a porn addict preaching sexual purity, we don't have the right to ask for people's money if we're going to keep ours pocketed.

Establish Controls

Executive overseers can serve the church well by building systems to ensure financial accountability. Not only is the reputation of the kingdom at stake, but if we can't be faithful with the little Jesus has given us, we can't expect him to entrust us with more.[40] Here are some examples of checks, balances, and financial controls that we have in place at Mars Hill:

- *Offering*: At least two people (i.e., non-family) must be with the offering at all times. The count is verified by at least three people.
- *Checks*: At least three people are involved in processing every check: requestor, approver, and signer.

---

39 Willard and Sheppard, *Contagious Generosity*, 79.
40 Luke 16:10; Matt. 25:14–30.

- *Lead Pastor*: The lead pastor never handles any of the offering or signs any checks and is generally far removed from any financial matters.
- *Certified Staff*: Our staff includes multiple CPAs and other qualified financial professionals.
- *Annual Audit*: At our own expense, each year we undergo a voluntary audit, administered by an external accounting firm.
- *Giving Communication*: We keep our congregation informed of our financial health with monthly giving updates and an annual report that includes our income statement and balance sheet for the year.
- *Spending*: Approved business-related expenses are outlined in detail in our staff operations manual, and larger purchases require approval and additional paperwork, such as a purchase requisition.
- *Credit Cards*: We limit the number of church credit cards issued, and staff use an online program to submit reimbursements and credit card reconciliations, which also go through multiple rounds of approval.
- *Compensation*: No one on staff sets his or her own salary, and we identify fair and reasonable compensation using a nationwide survey of comparable churches and ministries. Compensation for senior-level staff is determined by an independent board.
- *External Accountability*: We are accredited with the Evangelical Council for Financial Accountability, which publishes our financial information online for total visibility.

Some of these tactics may seem like overkill or irrelevant for smaller churches and organizations, but whether Jesus has given you a lot or a little, the call to be "above reproach" remains the same. Also, remember that it's much easier to establish healthy precedents when a church is small, rather than fix bad habits, leaky systems, and entitlement culture later on.

A few extra financial controls will instill trust within the congregation and protect the church from accusations. People will be more likely to give if they know that the money is being used and stewarded well. Ultimately, however, a church should be led by the Holy Spirit, not policy. "The image we need to have is of us sitting in front of the throne room of God," says my friend, Todd Lane, associate senior pastor at Gateway Church in Southlake, Texas. Then, when it comes time to make a financial decision, "we simply turn to God and ask him what we should do, and then we respond accordingly. The point is, we should use policies to guide us. But they should only be a guide."[41]

Fundraise

The Bible says, "Bread is made for laughter, and wine gladdens life, and money answers everything."[42] Whether or not King Solomon was exaggerating this point, the truth is we won't make it very far without money. Rather than treating money as a useful and necessary instrument for executing kingdom work, however, many pastors approach the topic with reluctance and apologies—if they address it at all. Willard and Jim describe the need for a "ministry of asking":

> In our conversations with hundreds of church members, it is clear to us that the church is missing a great opportunity. In many of these conversations, it's obvious that the church did not capture the heart of the giver

---

41 Todd Lane (Associate Senior Pastor, Gateway Church), in discussion with the author, April 2013.
42 Eccles. 10:19.

because the pastor never took the time to ask. . . . Think
about how much money fails to reach the offering plate,
instead going to other well-meaning organizations, all
because the church simply fails to ask.[43]

The difference between traditional fundraising and the ministry of
asking is the Holy Spirit. To paraphrase Tony Campolo, God has
already provided more than enough to meet the church's needs,
but much of it is still in the pews. Like the work of salvation, the
Holy Spirit will move people to respond; our job is to simply provide a clear call to action.

I had zero fundraising experience when I took on my first capital campaign as an executive pastor. What I discovered, however,
is that for the most part, it simply takes someone who is willing to
take the time and meet with people, answer questions, pray, make
the ask, and handle the follow-up. Here are some other practical
tips I've picked up through the years:

- **It's all about Jesus.** Don't start with the need. Start with
  Jesus—what he's doing, what he has done for us, and what
  he's calling us to do. Invite people to respond; don't cajole
  them out of guilt.
- **Win hearts.** Do your best to meet people where they're at,
  and tell the story of the need from an angle that appeals
  to them. Some people will care about how the project
  will help reach lost people and care for them. Others will
  want to make sure that the project is well organized, with
  a timeline, budget, and scope. Still others will want to
  understand how the effort aligns with God's overall vision
  for the church.

43 Willard and Sheppard, *Contagious Generosity*, 110–11.

- **Know your donors.** Review all of the donors at your church and identify the large donors and the faithful givers. This isn't about playing favorites, but just as every church has go-to volunteers always willing to show up and help out, every church also has go-to givers who are always eager to contribute to a worthy effort.
- **Answer questions.** Leaders must listen to questions. Even if it doesn't change what you're doing, you have to make a concerted effort to hear people out, in order to build trust and earn support.
- **Make the ask.** Regenerated believers want to participate in the kingdom of God by giving. Most people simply need some encouragement, direction, and a bold, straightforward, specific ask. People who like to give appreciate directness, and many enjoy a challenge as well.
- **Don't break it down.** If you need to raise about $400,000 and your church has 500 adults, the worst thing you can say is, "If everybody would just give $800, we'd reach our goal." Those who can't give $800 will feel left out. Maybe $100 was the sacrifice they had in mind, but now that amount hardly seems worthwhile. Also, for someone who had planned on giving $8,000, they'll likely reduce that amount because you just told them you only needed $800. It's OK to ask people to give a specific amount on an individual basis, but under any circumstance, giving to the church should be generous, cheerful, regular, and sacrificial, "according to what a person has."[44]
- **Make the call above and beyond.** At Mars Hill Church, we always make a point to say that giving to any sort of special fundraiser should be "above and beyond" normal,

44 2 Cor. 8:12.

regular church giving. We want to minimize redirected giving as much as possible. A new building doesn't do much good if your operating budget takes a 50 percent hit in the fundraising process.

- **Say "thank you."** When it's all said and done, be sure to follow up, say thanks, and celebrate the work God has done through his people. Send handwritten notes, make personal phone calls, and go the extra mile to show appreciation on behalf of the church and the mission of Jesus.

- **Share stories.** In any church fundraising campaign, there are usually a few miraculous examples of people stepping out in faith and God providing opportunities to give (e.g., a random check in the mail, an unexpected promotion, an anonymous donor, etc.) These stories will glorify God and go a long way in encouraging the church's faith.

- **Pray, pray, pray.** Talking about giving and asking people to contribute is spiritual warfare. Money is an idol Jesus called out by name.[45] Even if some people don't worship money specifically, it's probably connected to some other idol (e.g., a hobby, a car, a lifestyle) that takes precedence over the church. When we ask people to give, we may have no idea what the Holy Spirit is up to in their hearts.

- **Listen to the Holy Spirit.** Through prayer and obedience to the Holy Spirit, God will align church leadership, church membership, and church fundraising projects with his priorities. Todd Lane recalls a time in 2008 when Gateway was in the middle of a $100 million capital campaign and the economy began to tank. "Our elders met to discuss whether we were to put the project on hold until we saw the economic recovery. After prayer, we felt like God

---

45 Matt. 6:24.

was still saying to move forward. So we moved forward and completed the project under budget and ahead of schedule."[46]

Raising money is about so much more than generating cash. It's a beautiful illustration of the body of Christ at work: everyone does their part, and every part counts for something. It's amazing to see all of the ways God can use fundraising to build faith, change hearts, help people mature, and unite the church.

Disciple the Kings

As a new Christian and a successful businessman, I didn't think I could serve the church. My travel schedule made it hard to lead a small group or commit to a volunteer team, and I wasn't interested in doing "churchy" stuff like counseling or preaching. But then my pastor pointed out that giving is a spiritual gift.[47] I could give. A lot. But the thought had never crossed my mind that I could serve by giving. Once I saw it as an act of service, it gave me great joy to give to the church, and it opened my heart to participating in other ways.

"Many pastors instinctively know that they need to nurture, train, and develop people in the church who have the gifts of leading, serving, or teaching," says Pastor Robert Morris, who leads Gateway Church. "They will instruct them and help them learn to function better in their gifts. But many of the same pastors don't even know how to recognize the gift of giving as a spiritual gift, and if they do, they don't know how to help people grow in it."[48] Failure to recognize, cultivate, and encourage the gift of giving is

[46] Lane, discussion.

[47] Rom. 12:8.

[48] Robert Morris, *The Blessed Life: The Simple Secret of Achieving Guaranteed Financial Results* (Ventura, CA: Regal Books, 2002), 136.

not only a missed opportunity for the financial well-being of the church, it's also a missed opportunity for discipleship.

Pastors and churches discriminate against financially successful people, in large part due to the growing popularity of poverty theology that presumes an inverse relationship between godliness and net worth. In my experience, very few people in the ministry world can relate to their brothers and sisters living in the business world. In order to avoid the sin of partiality,[49] pastors leave the wealthy to fend for themselves. Willard and Sheppard describe the problem well:

> Because of their apparent success, we tend to assume that high-capacity people don't need a lot of attention from the church. We forget that they too need to be discipled and guided in their growth as Christ followers. Even though they have been successful in certain endeavors, they have all the same problems as other families in the church. They may have relationship conflicts with their children and spouses, they may have addictions they fight against, and they may suffer from spiritual malnourishment. . . .
>
> Jesus said it is easier for a camel to go through the eye of a needle than for a rich person to enter the kingdom of God. He singled out the wealthy as being at particularly high risk of missing the path to eternal life. As a pastor or church leader, this should be foremost in your mind. This is why it's important for the church to reach out to high-capacity men and women. They need to hear the gospel, and they need to grow spiritually—just like the rest of us.
>
> It's important that the relationship you cultivate with high-capacity people is based on more than what they have

---

49 James 2:1–9.

to offer you. Don't become just another person representing just another organization that wants a payday. In fact, if your only intention is to ask for something, you are likely to fail. And by violating their trust in the church, you could also do significant spiritual harm. Your desire for relationship should be based on a genuine concern for their spiritual well-being, for their growth and development as followers of Christ. Your interest in them is not just a tactic or ploy; it's a natural outgrowth of the church's commitment to lovingly serve people.[50]

I pray that God will use my story and the stories of other executive pastors to reach more business leaders for Jesus and call them to serve his mission. These folks generally don't connect well with a seminary graduate or a priest. But they love Jesus, they have money to give, and they have skills to use if only they knew how to apply them to a church context. What they need is a like-minded believer to come alongside them. Show them how the church is not a glorified soup kitchen but a family to love. Teach them about God's perspective on money. Pray for them. Disciple them. Relate to them. I know the struggles of corporate life. I can talk about how Jesus saved me from a life ruled by possessions. I can pray through business decisions and bring wisdom from my experience. I understand what it's like to live in a marriage frayed by years of selfish ambition. As an executive pastor, I can pastor executives.

The mechanism God used to shift my focus from my own kingdom to his kingdom was money. Understanding stewardship and the spiritual gift of giving was a pathway that led to service, growth, and maturity in my life. But I learned about giving in the context of a true friendship with a brother who cared about me.

---

[50] Willard and Sheppard, *Contagious Generosity*, 123–24.

Early on in our relationship, while I was still working in real estate, I told Pastor Joe about an important board meeting I had coming up. He promised to pray for me. This sounded like an empty pleasantry at the time, so it meant a great deal when I got a text message from him on the morning of the meeting, just to let me know he was praying.

Money is an important resource for the church, but it's connected to something infinitely more important: people. Whether it's mission, worship, repentance, discipleship, or some other form of heart change, ultimately money is just a means to a much greater, much more meaningful end.

CHAPTER EIGHT

PLAN FOR A FUTURE

I WAS DONE WITH THE MIDDLE EAST. After a couple of years living halfway around the world, I was ready for a break. I had left Texas to build businesses for one of Abu Dhabi's royal sheikhs. My family came along with me, and we had quite the adventure living in the Middle East and traveling the world. The money was great, but I could only do the expatriate thing for so long. Raising a family in a very foreign culture is difficult, and the spiritual climate was challenging, to say the least. The companies all adhered to Muslim principles and religious laws, and one of the board members I worked with was a known funder of the Taliban. The only Christian church around was of the out-of-control, flag-waving, prosperity-loving, slay-you-in-the-Spirit persuasion. We attended anyway, but every Sunday we'd also sit down as a family and watch the video podcast from a pastor in Seattle named Mark Driscoll.

I learned more and more about Mars Hill, and eventually the church began to feel like extended family. I visited the website often, and when I saw a job posting for Chief Financial Officer, I decided to apply. As it turns out, I had no idea what I was getting myself into. In early 2011 Mars Hill offered me a job as General Manager, and my family moved to Seattle shortly after. Our plan was to catch our breath, settle down, and enjoy a little margin in our lives to finalize the adoption of my son, who was still living in an orphanage in Ethiopia. After years of leading billion-dollar corporations at the speed of global commerce, my only concern was that I'd get bored pretty quick. God must have had a pretty good laugh over that one!

About six months after I started working at Mars Hill, the executive pastor resigned. There was nothing scandalous—he remained in church leadership as a volunteer pastor—but the decision was quite unexpected. At the time, I had only met Pastor Mark in passing, and now all of a sudden I found myself in the position of heir apparent for the second-in-charge slot. Jesus never asked me if I wanted *that* job.

So I got the keys and had to jump in the driver's seat while the car was still moving. I hadn't endured a full winter in the Pacific Northwest. I hadn't met everyone on the staff that I was now supposed to lead. I wasn't even a Mars Hill pastor yet. I was still very much the new guy. I had a lot of authority and no influence, which is a very tough spot for a leader. To make matters worse, I had come to find out I had inherited an organization that had outgrown its systems long ago and a lead pastor on the verge of a breakdown, just as the church was gearing up for its biggest growth surge ever. God has called me to do some crazy things in my life, but nothing quite like those first couple of years at Mars Hill.

I pray that my experience is an anomaly. But hopefully it can serve as an exaggerated example of what's to come for you, should God call you to step into a role like executive pastor. Chances are some of the rocks you turn over will be hiding a gnarled, slimy mess underneath—especially if your church has never had executive oversight. In this chapter, I hope to provide a general framework to help you assess the damage and help your church get on track for a healthy future.

The Next Level

Everything you've ever heard about high school football in Texas is true. In my teenage world, playing on the team was unquestionably more important than academics and certainly more fun. But I received a rude awakening every year around November, about the time when the season ended and I finally started paying attention in math class. Every lesson built upon a previous concept, which means my rate of ignorance was increasing at an exponential rate (not that I could have explained exponents, since I missed that lecture).

You've gotta learn arithmetic before you can move on to algebra. You've gotta learn algebra before you can move on to trigonometry. You've gotta learn trigonometry before you can move on to calculus. You get the idea. Learning is more than simply taking in new information; it's a progressive development that builds on previous knowledge. It's moving on and starting over in an area that's newer, harder, and more complicated than before. My fellow Texan, Pastor Ed Young Jr. calls it "a whole 'nother level," and it applies in ministry and in life.[1]

---

1 I'm indebted to both Ed Young Jr. and T. D. Jakes for many of the principles that I'm building on in this chapter.

Growth requires a conscious effort to reach the next level, both as an individual and an organization. It helps to think of this effort like a staircase:

Level Three	1	2	3	4	5	6	7	8	9	10
Level Two	1	2	3	4	5	6	7	8	9	10
Level One	1	2	3	4	5	6	7	8	9	10

Every person, every church, every organization is somewhere on the staircase, based on skills, experience, education, size, etc. A different staircase exists for your marriage, your personal growth, your family, your career, your business, etc. Furthermore, at any given step on the staircase, we're all somewhere on the continuum between one and nine. (Only Jesus gets a ten.) A brand new father is a "1" on the very first level of parenting. He doesn't even know how to change a diaper. A grandfather, however, has brought up kids from the childhood level through the teenage level, through the grown-up level. He's endured and enjoyed the full spectrum of fatherhood.

The "next level" could be a new job, a promotion, a baby in the family, a growth milestone, or any number of transitions. Sometimes the step up is drastic and clear; other times it's more of a gradual incline. Either way, you'll know you've reached a new level when your old way of doing things isn't working anymore. Systems break, processes fail, relationships strain, chaos ensues. That's exactly what happened at Mars Hill. The church had grown to over 10,000 in weekly attendance, with 14 locations in four different states. And yet, the organizational structure and systems were essentially the same as they'd been five years prior. We didn't do a good job of anticipating the changes needed at the next level.

Growth brings change. That's true for big churches and small churches, and it's true for people, families, corporations, countries, whatever. In some cases, you're going to the next level whether you like it or not—as in physical maturity, for example. In other cases, it's a more deliberate journey. Either way, if you want to function at the next level, reinvention is absolutely necessary.

Six Keys for Reinvention

When a family starts having kids, a lot of reinvention takes place. New parents need to figure out what life looks like with less personal time and more demands. Another bedroom, a larger car, or a different neighborhood might be in order. The church family is similar. An increase in attendance, a new service time, or a different location all require more volunteers, more detailed planning, a different communication strategy, and other adjustments. For fast growing churches, reinvention is necessary for survival. For static churches, reinvention is an opportunity to reinvigorate the mission for another push forward. Either way, many of the considerations are the same.

1. Start with the leader

When change is required or desired, it must start with the leader. This is especially true in a church, where the lead pastor's vision, strengths, and style wield a great deal of influence through the ministry of preaching. When Mark Driscoll turned 40, he took deliberate steps to transition from young-gun preacher to fatherly pastor. He never stopped preaching the Bible, but his tone, his wardrobe, and his emphases all began to change. This shift sent a message throughout the church body, that we were done with our childhood years and needed to move toward full maturity.

Change for the leader isn't just about aesthetics. When Mars Hill Church was in the midst of crisis, Pastor Dave Bruskas, my fellow second-in-charge, and I spent a lot of time focusing on Pastor Mark's workload in order to alleviate pain points and help get him to a place of health. The reinvention process starts with the leader not only because he drives the vision but because the rest of the organization will be in trouble if the leader doesn't make it. Once the leader is in a good place, it's much easier to reinvent the systems and structure of the organization—which is what the rest of this section is primarily about.

2. Define the next level

For churches, the most obvious next-level marker is attendance. As we discussed earlier on, if a church of 200 wants to become a church of 500, the lead pastor will probably need some sort of executive oversight to help make that jump. By no means is attendance the only way to measure progress, but if a church doubles in size, it will be on a new level in terms of its need for volunteers, a system for assimilating new people, more small groups, better communication, and someone to architect all of those adjustments. Besides attendance, a church may experience a new transition when a new leader takes over, when the congregation moves to a new building, or when young families start having kids, for example.

A church that waits for the next level to arrive before taking on these tasks will either be caught unprepared—like me in math class—or the lack of initiative will become a self-fulfilling prophecy, with the church ceasing to grow and mature. Though you don't want to get too far ahead of yourself, especially when it comes to spending, if you fail to make the changes at your current level, you'll probably never get to the next one.

3. Start all over

The things that make a good supervisor are not the same things that make a good manager. Neither are they the same things that make a good CEO. Likewise, success for a new church starting out in the pastor's living room will look much different when that church moves into the community center, and once again when they buy their first building.

It's helpful to think about this process on a personal level. I started my first business right out of business school. I didn't have any practical business experience, so I was at the very beginning—level one, stage one. Over the next eight years, however, I made progress by getting various certifications, attending conferences, meeting with mentors, and learning from my mistakes. A few years later, I started over again when I moved to the Middle East. Wheeling and dealing in Texas wasn't quite the same as doing business in Abu Dhabi. I was working with billions of dollars and thousands of employees rather than millions and hundreds. Plus, I had to start from scratch and learn the basics related to global culture, context, and codes.

For a church, starting over may include scrapping certain programs, drafting a new governance system, creating a new budget model, and in other ways rebuilding the infrastructure so that it can bear the future load.

4. Stay humble and learn

Success at a previous level does not guarantee success at the next level. Never assume you're an expert on level five because you were an expert on level four. The game at the next level is harder, which means you have to step it up in order to succeed. Stay humble. Instead of comparing yourself to others, seek to learn from them instead. Success has nothing to do with how many levels you climb. Rather, it's measured by personal growth, maturity, sanctification, mission, and faithful stewardship. Pride pursues the next level in order to be the best and enjoys seeing others fall a few steps back. Humility pursues the next level in order to be faithful and fruitful, and enjoys helping others move a few steps forward.

A beautiful example of humble leadership took place when Mars Hill Church announced plans to start a new location in Tacoma, about an hour south of our established territory in Seattle. The lead pastor at another church in Tacoma sent a letter to welcome us and encourage us. "This is an answer to the prayers of many followers of Jesus," wrote Pastor Dean Curry. "Jesus has just one church in Tacoma! When someone comes to our city lifting Jesus up, we know they are part of that one church." He went on to offer friendship, people, and money, as an act of solidarity and celebration for God's work in the city.

Mars Hill Church and Life Center Church are on two different "levels" of ministry, and on paper it would appear that Mars Hill has the leg up. We could coast into Tacoma and pridefully assume that everything will fall into place simply because we've experienced some success elsewhere. Likewise, Life Center could have resisted the new kid in town, guarded their territory, and resented the attention we received just for showing up. But God has called and equipped Mars Hill to do one thing, and God has called and equipped Life Center to do another. Same basic mission, different spheres and strengths. We have a lot to learn from them, and they might be able to learn some things from us.

Find someone who is a few steps ahead of where you want to be, drop them a line, ask questions, and learn. And look for opportunities to do the same for someone else.

5. Expect failures and mistakes

Progress inevitably includes failure, which is why many people and many churches stay put. It's far easier and far less scary to stick to what you've got and know and slip into maintenance mode.

Without new challenges, however, new growth will cease. Try, fail, and at least you'll end up learning something. Never try, never fail, and you'll probably end up full of regret and bitterness against those who took a risk that paid off. Going to the next level most likely involves great pain, great humility, and great failure, but it all comes with the possibility of great fruit as the payoff.

"If you want to innovate for Jesus, you have to say, Failure is not an option. Failure is a necessity." Craig Groeschel, author and lead pastor of LifeChurch.tv, illustrates his point by describing his church's first attempt at creating multiple sites. The team had prayed about it and truly believed it was God's will, but the result was a total flop. Rather than giving up, however, they learned from the experience. "We realized that the key to doing multisite ministry is not in the technology, it's not in the preaching, but it's always in the development of people—leadership." He tells another story about the church's wildly popular YouVersion Bible app. It started out as a social media website that failed, but "you try something, you fail, you learn, and you adjust."[2]

Preparing for the next level is a healthy exercise, even if the transition is a long way off. It forces people to think about what's working and what's not, rather than settling for the status quo. Sometimes, the preparation itself can become a catalyst that sparks maturity and growth. As the lead pastor calls people to a vision of a destination, a strategic-thinking executive pastor figures out how to get there, level by level.

---

[2] Craig Groeschel, Resurgence Conference, Irvine, CA, October 10, 2012.

Helping Your Church Get There

Three factors will fuel or foil your church's journey to the next level of size and maturity. Every church of every size must evaluate each one of these three variables in order to remain healthy in the present and plan for the future. All three are vital but have varying degrees of importance—(from least to greatest) money, leaders, and Jesus.

Variable #1: Money

Growth is expensive. More people require more accommodations, more services, more square footage, more pastoral care, and just plain more of everything. To further complicate things, new people usually don't show up and start giving right away. A best-case scenario would see a thousand people show up, drink the coffee, use the bathroom, fill a seat, meet Jesus, schedule a counseling appointment, and generally hang out for a few months before giving a dime. It's a beautiful problem to have, but it does present an interesting challenge if you're financially unprepared.

I won't belabor the point here, since we've already addressed the subject in the previous chapter, but suffice it to say, without a budget, fundraising plan, donor communication strategy—without money—a church will struggle to achieve and/or survive the next level.

Variable #2: Leaders

One pastor cannot take care of a church by himself. One lead pastor and one executive pastor cannot take care of a church together. The church must take care of the church. Consultant and former executive pastor David Fletcher reminds us, "The role of the pastor is to equip the people of God for ministry. Most churches do a horrendous job at that." No matter the size, a church needs some sort of "leadership pipeline" that can guide people through the process of first-time guest to committed member. For example:

1. *Volunteers.* If somebody shows up at church on a Sunday and decides to get involved, find a way to put them to work on the spot. Not only is their service helpful to the church, but it's also a great way for new people to meet others and start building relationships.

2. *Members.* Without a proper understanding, membership can make church sound like an exclusive club. But the concept derives from the Bible's metaphor of the church as a body: "For the body does not consist of one member but of many."[3] Nobody has to take a class or get a certificate to be included in the body of Christ, but an official membership process is a way to demonstrate how the church is not just a Sunday event but a functioning organism that requires committed members acting in concert. A call to membership is a call to take ownership by caring for the well-being of the entire body.

3. *Deacons.* Deacons are the men and women who take on the work of day-to-day ministry, allowing the overseers to devote their time "to prayer and to the ministry of the word." Deacons hold an official spiritual office defined by Scripture.[4] Deacons generally take on more responsibility and must demonstrate a higher standard of spiritual maturity in order to lead small groups, ministry teams, and administrative tasks.

4. *Overseers.* The Bible identifies the role of overseer as the highest human authority within the local church, whose

---

3 1 Cor. 12:14.
4 1 Tim. 3:8–13.

responsibility it is "to care for the church of God."[5] The role is translated and described in various ways, including *pastor*, *elder*, and *shepherd*, in addition to *overseer*. Overseers lead other leaders and the church overall.

These four categories represent a basic, biblical framework for leadership growth within the church. From brand-new Christian to mature believer, this leadership pipeline provides a place to start and some next-level goals for everyone on the spectrum.

Even at a large church, the majority of leaders will be unpaid volunteers, including deacons and elders. The leadership pipeline is not a career track but a chance for people to worship Jesus, care for his people, and grow in spiritual maturity.

In addition to leadership development, a church must also consider the right leadership structure. Larry Osborne uses a series of sports metaphors to describe how leadership structure must change as a church grows: The evolution begins with the track star, one leader who does everything. Once a few more people start helping out, the operation resembles a foursome on the golf course—very relational and informal. Eventually it's time for basketball—larger teams with specialized positions. A large church plays football with a team of teams led by numerous coaches connected by more complex, formal lines of communication.[6] "The need to change the game, as well as the rules of the game, tends to sneak up on leaders and leadership teams because growth exponentially increases complexity," says Osborne. "We might think that we've only *added* a couple of new programs or staff members, but in reality, we've *multiplied* organizational complexity."[7]

---

5 Acts 20:28.
6 Larry Osborne, *Sticky Teams*, 63–66.
7 Ibid., 70.

An executive pastor can love his church well by thinking through these organizational dilemmas and working with the lead pastor to develop a game plan that creates relational margin and leadership capacity to welcome, disciple, help, and reach more people. If leadership isn't healthy and growing, the church won't be healthy and growing either. Yet, we must keep in mind that the right structure and pipeline isn't the magic formula to a bigger church. Only Jesus can make it grow.

Variable #3: Jesus

In the business world, it's easy to manage results, measure activities against the bottom line, and generally maintain some illusion of control. The church could benefit from a dose of executive experience, but if you plan on bringing that to the table, prepare for a paradigm shift. We are servants and stewards of our Father's business—he is in charge.

The Apostle Paul said it well: "Neither he who plants nor he who waters is anything, but only God who gives the growth."[8] When it comes to the future of the church and thinking about whether or not it's going to the next level, we can plan, prepare, develop, strategize, manage, administrate, and oversee all we want. But we can't make it happen. On the surface, this revelation may discourage the ambitious, results-driven audience that I'm hoping will read this book. From one highly driven individual to another, however, I assure you, this is good news. Jesus was emphatic: "I will build my church."[9] We can do our best, work hard, and trust God's purpose will prevail—even when we screw up.

God's sovereign power is not only tremendously liberating but also spiritually healthy. If you've experienced any amount of

---

[8] 1 Cor. 3:7.
[9] Matt. 16:18.

success in the worlds of business, real estate, and money, it's easy to think you're the man. You're not the man. You're not your performance. You're not your net worth. You're not your job title. If you belong to Jesus, the only aspect of your identity that really, truly, eternally matters is that of redeemed child of God. We're helpless without him. That's as true in the corporate world as it is in the ministry world. But there's something about serving the church that makes this reality all the more poignant.

Jesus loves the church more than anything else in the entire world. She is his bride, and to think that he would entrust her well-being in part to my care is daunting. I could not accept the responsibility unless I knew that Jesus was all in. And he is. He didn't die for Apple, Google, or KPMG—or Young Life, World Vision, or Compassion International, for that matter. Jesus died for the church. The church represents the tip of the spear of God's work in the world. Talk about significance—I want in on that business! I would take any role I could get just to be a part of it, but the fact that he's equipped me and called me to actually oversee some of the effort is an incredible privilege that blows my mind. I get to be an executive pastor. Thank you, Jesus! There's no job I'd rather do in the whole world.

Will you join me?

PART THREE:

GOOD COMPANY

Stories from the Field

CHAPTER NINE

WE GO WAY BACK

YOU'VE HEARD THE NEED. You've heard the call. You're not alone.

Maybe the whole notion of serving your church as an executive overseer still sounds kind of crazy. Would God really ask someone to give up all of their Sunday mornings or commit career suicide? I hope by now you can accept that such outcomes are within the realm of possibility, but even if you're leaning in that direction, I don't expect it will be an easy decision. Therefore, in this final section, I'd like to share a few stories with you of business-minded men whom God used to bless his people and build his kingdom. I want to show you some ways that God has worked in the lives of others to help you recognize how he might work in yours.

Throughout this book, I've included select quotes and

anecdotes from other executive pastors. In this section, I will
share extended excerpts from my conversations with some
of these men, edited for clarity and space. These conversations were incredibly beneficial and encouraging to me personally, and I imagine other executive pastors and would-be
executive pastors could gain a lot from others whose wisdom
and experience far outweighs my own. I am extremely grateful
to these men for allowing me to bring their voices into the pages
of this book.

But before we learn from our contemporary brothers, let's
take a look at our spiritual heritage and the biblical precedent
for offering up our business talent in service to God.

A Great Cloud of Witnesses and a Handful of Scoundrels

The Bible is first and foremost the story of God's effort to redeem
his creation, rescue his people, and reveal his splendor and goodness
as the King of kings in the person of Jesus Christ. We completely
miss the purpose of the Book when we reduce it to a legalistic set
of rules to obey or a series of illustrations to live by. Having said
that, God does work through human lives in part so that we may
learn from others' example, both positive and negative.[1]

You won't find any "executive pastors" in the Bible, but its
pages contain many examples of individuals equipped with skills
to organize, manage, administrate, and lead. Some use their talents to the glory of God and the benefit of his people, while
others operate with a more selfish goal in mind. Far more could
be said about the context and the meaning of the lives of these
men, their actions, and how they fit into the bigger picture of the
grand narrative of God's story. But for the purposes of this little

---

[1] Heb. 12:1; cf. 1 Cor. 10:11.

book, I'd like to simply introduce you to a few of these historical characters, provide a brief synopsis of their lives, and propose a few lessons we may learn from their examples. In other words, consider this a quick roll call for some of the Bible's businessmen. By no means is the list or these summaries meant to be exhaustive. I encourage you to study further to get the full effect. In the meantime, this will give you some idea of the ways God has worked through executive leaders, seconds-in-charge, and other like-minded folks.

Joseph

> Then Pharaoh said to Joseph, "Since God has shown
> you all this, there is none so discerning and wise
> as you are. You shall be over my house, and all my
> people shall order themselves as you command. Only
> as regards the throne will I be greater than you."
> (Genesis 41:39–40)

Joseph was a brash dreamer, sold into slavery by his jealous brothers. Through servitude and imprisonment, Joseph grew in humility, experience, and leadership. Separated from his family and literally stripped of his most treasured possession, Joseph had every reason to sink into bitter oblivion. Instead, Joseph chose dependence on God. Through a series of providential events, God called him to serve as the second-in-charge to the most powerful ruler in the ancient world, Pharaoh. Joseph used his managerial skills to prepare Egypt for impending famine. Thanks to Joseph's stewardship, the nation averted catastrophe and God's people were preserved.

One of the principles we see at work in the life of Joseph is that loyalty breeds loyalty. Before anyone else, Joseph knew that the land would experience seven years of plenty followed by seven years of lack. Though he could have exploited this tip for his own gain, Joseph used the information to faithfully steward the nation's resources for the benefit of the people and his leader. He was 100 percent focused on Pharaoh's interests, not on his own. At one point, "Joseph gathered up all the money that was found in the land of Egypt and the land of Canaan, in exchange for the grain that they bought. And Joseph brought the money into Pharaoh's house."[2] Pharaoh recognized Joseph's loyalty and, in turn, cared for him and trusted him completely.[3]

Though Joseph's loyalty was evident in his relationship with Pharaoh, ultimately it was an overflow of his desire to remain faithful to God. We see this throughout the story. Joseph had the opportunity to sleep with his boss's wife. He refused, out of love for God. Joseph had the opportunity to take credit for his dream interpretation skills. Instead he gave credit to God. Joseph had the opportunity to win power from Pharaoh. He chose to save the country and rescue people from starvation instead. Joseph had the opportunity to retaliate against his brothers who betrayed him and sold him into slavery. He decided to forgive them because, as he reminded them, "You meant evil against me, but God meant it for good."[4]

Joseph's heart was tested over and over. Over and over, it beat for the Lord. Joseph existed for something greater than earthly pleasure, comfort, or fame. And while Joseph's achievements in the face of adversity were astounding, "The Lord was with Joseph and showed him steadfast love and gave him favor."[5]

[2] Gen. 47:14.
[3] Gen. 41:55.
[4] Gen. 50:20.
[5] Gen. 39:21.

Joseph would have been the first to recognize that God, not he, was the hero of this story, and we are equally dependent on his grace and mercy.

Jethro

> Moses' father-in-law said to him, "What you are doing is not good. You and the people with you will certainly wear yourselves out, for the thing is too heavy for you. You are not able to do it alone. Now obey my voice; I will give you advice, and God be with you!" (Exodus 18:17–19)

Moses had become spent. After years of leading God's people on a circuitous journey through the Middle Eastern wilderness, he was stuck in the weeds—in meetings all day, listening to grievances, and generally trying to keep thousands of grumpy Israelites from turning on the God who had supernaturally intervened to deliver them from slavery.

On one occasion, Moses' father-in-law, Jethro, dropped in on the nomad nation for a visit. He noticed that Moses was single-handedly serving the entire people group as personal arbitrator. "The people come to me to inquire of God," Moses explained. "When they have a dispute, they come to me and I decide between one person and another, and I make them know the statutes of God and his laws."[6] Jethro immediately recognized that this arrangement was not sustainable. He suggested that Moses delegate the task to "men who fear God, who are trustworthy and hate a bribe."[7] It's a simple, clear plan that allowed Moses to reclaim hours, if not years of his life—time he probably spent writing the first five books of the Bible.

---

[6] Exod. 18:15–16.
[7] Exod. 18:21.

In Jethro's example, we see the invaluable contribution an older, more experienced leader can provide, especially one who arrives with independent perspective. Jethro was well established in his life with his own tribe and his own concerns. He was able to offer Moses genuine care and advice because he didn't need anything from Moses (e.g., status, validation, employment). Also, he served Moses for a very brief season. Jethro helped him establish a few key systems and then moved on. He wasn't called to one church and one leader for all time; God used him in a particular moment to make an impact that would last more than a lifetime.

In this way, Jethro is an excellent model for seasoned business leaders within the church. You may not have the time and energy to devote to a full-time executive/overseer role, but when used strategically according to your gifts, you can be like a bullet from a sniper rifle—not a lot of rounds, but each shot is much more likely to do some positive damage.

Aaron

> And the Lord said to Moses, "See, I have made you like God to Pharaoh, and your brother Aaron shall be your prophet. You shall speak all that I command you, and your brother Aaron shall tell Pharaoh to let the people of Israel go out of his land." (Exodus 7:1–2)

Jethro wasn't the only other leader involved in Moses' ministry. God had called Moses to confront Pharaoh and demand the liberation of God's people, but due to Moses' reluctance to fulfill the task, God appointed Aaron to serve alongside his brother. Aaron, the second-in-charge, is one of those characters in the Bible who's not exactly heroic but not quite a villain either. In other words, he was kind of a regular guy who was in over his head and experienced both wins and losses along the way. Aaron stood firm next to Moses in the presence of Pharaoh, but in the wilderness he caved in to the Israelites' demands to build them a golden calf to worship in place of God.

In Aaron's life, we see the significance of what it means to be called to the 2IC role and the importance of being obedient to one's calling. Aaron was anointed high priest to serve alongside Moses, and the Bible is clear that "no one takes this honor for himself, but only when called by God, just as Aaron was."[8] So long as Aaron remained faithful in the 2IC slot by following the vision God had given to Moses, it went pretty well. God used Aaron to make a powerful impression in front of Pharaoh, and in another memorable scene, Aaron stood alongside Moses to help him keep his arms raised during battle—a powerful illustration of 2IC leadership.[9]

It was when Aaron drifted from his divinely appointed role that he began to get into trouble. As the *New Bible Dictionary* records, "On the one occasion when he acted independently of Moses' instructions he acted wrongly" (the aforementioned golden calf incident).[10] Later on in the story, Aaron and his sister jealously remark, "Has the Lord indeed spoken only through Moses? Has he not spoken through us also?"[11] They wanted to contribute to the vision. They wanted the kind of influence Moses enjoyed. They coveted his calling, rather than obeyed their own. So God literally showed up and issued a strong rebuke, and Aaron responded with genuine repentance.

---

[8] Heb. 5:4.
[9] Exod. 17:11–13.
[10] "Aaron," F.F. Bruce, *New Bible Dictionary* (Leicester, England: InterVarsity Press, 1996), 1.
[11] Num. 12:2.

His mistakes were grievous, but in this way Aaron served as a realistic example of what it looks like to experience both lows and highs while following another leader's God-given vision. I'm not surprised Aaron struggled with submitting to his own kid brother, but the fact that Aaron remained with him and God's people until the end is a testament to his character and, most of all, God's grace.

Haman

> King Ahasuerus promoted Haman the Agagite, the son of Hammedatha, and advanced him and set his throne above all the officials who were with him. And all the king's servants who were at the king's gate bowed down and paid homage to Haman, for the king had so commanded concerning him. (Esther 3:1–2)

Like Joseph, Haman was second-in-charge to the most powerful ruler in the known world, Ahasuerus (a.k.a. Xerxes), king of Persia. Unlike Joseph, however, Haman did not care about the people, the nation, or the king, let alone God. All that mattered to him was his own preeminence and rise to power. One subject of the kingdom, Mordecai, refused to pay homage to Haman, so Haman convinced the king to permit the extermination of Mordecai's people, the Jews. The king initially agreed to the plan, but when Queen Esther revealed that she herself was a Jew, Haman was executed.

King Ahasuerus is portrayed in the book of Esther as insecure, weak, self-serving, and ineffective. In other words, he was a leader with no shortage of weaknesses. Rather than serving the king by helping him recognize blind spots, Haman exploited the king's weakness in order to push his own agenda. Haman's big project was to use his position of power to strike the Jews, not because they represented any threat to Persia but because Haman carried a generational grudge against Mordecai and what he represented.[12] By manipulating his boss with the promise of great wealth, Haman convinced the king to legalize the genocide of God's people.

Haman promoted himself, his own vision, and his own interests well above the best interests of the king and the empire. When he reflected on his day at work, Haman didn't consider meaningful civic progress. Rather, he gathered together his wife and friends and recounted "to them the splendor of his riches, the number of his sons, all the promotions with which the king had honored him, and how he had advanced him above the officials and the servants of the king."[13] Haman only cared about his agenda, and the only thing on his agenda was Haman.

In many ways, Haman was the complete opposite of Joseph. While Joseph remained loyal even to the point of great personal cost, Haman was willing to undermine anyone in order to get what he wanted. Joseph's loyalty bred loyalty; Haman's disloyalty bred disloyalty. When things started to go bad for him, it's no surprise that everyone in his life, from the king, the queen, and even his own wife, turned on him. Nobody came to his defense when the king ordered his execution, and nobody was particularly sad to watch him go. Nobody cared about Haman because Haman cared about nobody.

Mordecai

And Mordecai came before the king, for Esther had told what he was to her. And the king took off his signet

---

[12] Esther 3:8–11; 6:4.
[13] Esther 5:11.

ring, which he had taken from Haman, and gave it to
Mordecai. And Esther set Mordecai over the house of
Haman. (Esther 8:1–2)

Haman's nemesis, Mordecai, was the cousin and caretaker
of Esther, the Jewish woman who became queen of Persia.
Mordecai worked in the courts of King Ahasuerus, and he
refused to acknowledge Haman's authority. Whether it was
an act of insolence or righteous civil disobedience, in God's
providence, things turned out well for Mordecai. After the
execution of Haman, the king named Mordecai as Haman's
replacement.

Like all human characters in the Bible, Mordecai was not
without his flaws. He was opportunistic to the extent that he was
willing to compromise the safety and well-being of his adopted
daughter Esther. But he demonstrated a number of admirable
attributes as well. Mordecai uncovered a plot to murder the king,
and though his good deed went unrecognized for years, he continued to serve the king faithfully and humbly. He also stood up
to the would-be tyrant Haman and protected God's people from
harm. He ended up in the same role as Haman, but rather than
use his status for personal benefit, Mordecai "sought the welfare
of his people and spoke peace to all his people."[14]

Mordecai was also an example of what it might look like to
serve as second-in-charge to a difficult leader. Obviously, his job
working for a reckless, pagan monarch was (hopefully) much
different from the circumstances found in church leadership. But
if Mordecai could influence a capricious dictator through tact,
humility, and respect, without resorting to subterfuge or manip-
ulation, there's hope for 2ICs everywhere. The case of Mordecai

---

[14] Esther 10:3.

leaves us no excuse to harbor bitterness or anger against the leaders we serve.

Nehemiah

> So in the lowest parts of the space behind the wall, in open places, I stationed the people by their clans, with their swords, their spears, and their bows. And I looked and arose and said to the nobles and to the officials and to the rest of the people, "Do not be afraid of them. Remember the Lord, who is great and awesome, and fight for your brothers, your sons, your daughters, your wives, and your homes." (Nehemiah 4:13–14)

The book of Nehemiah is arguably the greatest, most thorough example we have of biblical administrative leadership. It provides a first-person account of the life and times of Nehemiah, cupbearer to the king of Persia. With the glory days of Israel long behind, Nehemiah lived among God's people in exile. At this point in history, a small number had been granted permission to return to Jerusalem. When Nehemiah found out that the remnant was not faring well and that the city of Jerusalem had fallen into disrepair, he was deeply grieved. The king generously granted him a leave of absence, along with a number of resources, and Nehemiah set off to turn things around. Under his leadership as governor, the people of Jerusalem rebuilt the city wall and rediscovered a love for God's Word and a hope in God's promises.

A lot could be said about Nehemiah. For starters, he cared deeply for the same things that God did: God's people, God's reign, God's city, and God's law. Nehemiah wept, mourned, prayed, and fasted when he first heard about the sad state of affairs in Jerusalem. As a leader, he took responsibility for his people's neglect, though the state of his homeland was no direct fault of his own. He recognized his complicit role in the matter and indicted himself in his prayer of confession, crying out to God, "We have sinned against you. Even I and my father's house have sinned."[15] Once Nehemiah was on the ground in Jerusalem, he boldly confronted relentless opposition, logistical hardship, and overall complacency in the people. He governed with firm confidence, yet retained a deep love for the people, revealed by the fact that he decided to forego the governor's stipend and many other benefits of the office "because the service was too heavy on this people."[16]

In addition, Nehemiah continued to work within his gifting. He introduced many practical reforms, civic and religious, but when the time came for someone to get up and preach, Nehemiah deferred to Ezra, the scribe, and the priests. Time and time again, we see Nehemiah having gone out of his way to place the mission and the people before himself, to the glory of his "gracious and merciful God."[17] As one commentator notes, Nehemiah was "above all, a leader who was the opposite of a self-made man, one who was always conscious of the 'good hand' and the 'fear' of his God upon him."[18]

I'm sure some people in his day considered Nehemiah to be an overly intense taskmaster. But at a time when the nation of Israel was in total decay and nobody was doing anything about it, Nehemiah flat out cared. In case you haven't noticed, the state of the church today in the Western world is much like that of fifth-century-BC Jerusalem—disorganized, desolate, and disinterested. We could use

[15] Neh. 1:6.
[16] Neh. 5:18.
[17] Neh. 9:31.
[18] "Nehemiah, Book of," D. J. A. Clines, *New Bible Dictionary*, 814. With references to Neh. 2:8; 5:15; cf. 2:12, 18; 4:9, 14–15, 20; 6:9.

a few more Nehemiahs to model repentance and whip things into shape so that the Word of God can continue to bear fruit.

Judas

> Judas Iscariot, one of his disciples (he who was about to betray him), said, "Why was this ointment not sold for three hundred denarii and given to the poor?" He said this, not because he cared about the poor, but because he was a thief, and having charge of the moneybag he used to help himself to what was put into it. (John 12:4–6)

The closest example we see to a modern-day executive pastor in the Bible is Jesus' wayward disciple, Judas. Judas did not serve as second-in-charge, but he was included on Jesus' senior leadership team, the twelve disciples. Judas was an executive pastor prototype in that he reported to Jesus and was responsible for stewarding the group's financial resources. Not only did he steal from the fund, he eventually betrayed Jesus outright for thirty pieces of silver. After the notorious deed was done, Judas was awash with guilt. But rather than repent of his crime, he gave in to despair and took his own life.

Much speculation exists regarding Judas Iscariot's decision to betray Jesus. Whatever evil was brewing in Judas' heart, he clearly did not buy into Jesus' vision. Judas either did not trust, did not agree with, did not believe, did not like, or simply did not care about Jesus and his mission. This divergence didn't happen over-night. Judas followed Jesus for a few years. He had to have been drawn to the man for some initial reason, but those reasons very likely had to do with whatever Judas was hoping to get out of the relationship, not what Jesus had come to earth to accomplish.

This disconnect between where Jesus was going and where Judas wanted to go caused turmoil that eventually exploded into outright conflict and destruction.

Regardless of any other motives that may have led Judas to act, the Bible does make one thing absolutely clear: Judas loved money. He was the only disciple from Judea, a region that encompassed the big city of Jerusalem, so perhaps he was appointed treasurer because he understood commerce and finance. Maybe Judas was a businessman. In any case, "having charge of the moneybag he used to help himself to what was put into it."[19]

Judas' greed emerged again when he agreed to betray Jesus. "What will you give me if I deliver him over to you?" he asked the chief priests.[20] The prize that Judas accepted had nothing to do with political arrangements, power plays, or cloak-and-dagger insurrection—just cold, hard cash. Judas was called to use his gifts to help steward the resources of Jesus' ministry, and in the end, he found money to be more enticing than God himself. Judas interacted with two different lords on a daily basis, and he chose to worship the wrong one.

How much is Jesus worth to you? How much would you accept in exchange for turning your back on him? A six-figure salary? A comfortable house? A promotion? A lucrative business opportunity? Before we condemn Judas for his unabashed greed, it's important to take an honest look at ourselves and consider where we have chosen to pursue money, wealth, and possessions more zealously than the mission, vision, and person of Jesus.

The first executive pastor in the history of the church was a crook and a traitor. What a sobering, humbling heritage for those in this line of work. Through the infamy of Judas, God sends a

---

[19] John 12:6.
[20] Matt. 26:15.

warning to all future executive pastors: the lure of greed, money, influence, and power are great, and Satan will use these temptations in an effort to destroy us and our church.

Jesus

> "Truly, truly, I say to you, the Son can do nothing of his own accord, but only what he sees the Father doing. For whatever the Father does, that the Son does likewise." (John 5:19)

Besides Judas, the Gospels include at least one more example that executive pastors should find helpful and considerably more hopeful. "Few books on leadership emphasize the concepts of subordination, adding value for the benefit of others, and developing influence without formal authority," Bonem and Patterson write. "But this is exactly the style of leadership that is modeled by Jesus and repeatedly taught in the New Testament."[21]

The Father, the Son, and the Holy Spirit are each fully God, but throughout Scripture, Jesus demonstrated incredible respect, deference, and submission to his heavenly Father. "While the persons of the Trinity are equal in all their attributes," Dr. Wayne Grudem explains, "they nonetheless differ in their relationships to the creation. The Son and Holy Spirit are equal in deity to God the Father, but they are subordinate in their roles."[22]

This was especially apparent during Jesus' incarnation as a human being and earthly ministry. Everything he accomplished unfolded under the guidance and direction of God the Father. "I do nothing on my own authority, but speak just as the Father taught me," he says.[23] Like an executive pastor working with a lead pastor, Jesus worked according to the vision of another

---

[21] Bonem and Patterson, *Leading from the Second Chair*, 7.
[22] Wayne Grudem, *Systematic Theology*, 249.
[23] John 8:28.

leader. Jesus even suggested there were details of the Father's plan that he didn't know: "But concerning that day and hour no one knows, not even the angels of heaven, nor the Son, but the Father only."[24]

Jesus operated on behalf of his lead pastor, so to speak, and he continues to do so faithfully. "My food is to do the will of him who sent me," Jesus said, "and to accomplish his work."[25] Jesus loves his lead pastor, trusts him in life and even in death, and with fixed gaze followed the vision set before him.[26] Jesus is a strong leader who is completely sold out for another leader's vision. Though the concepts of submission and authority have fallen out of favor in our culture, including our churches, Jesus has no such qualms. It is his great joy to glorify the Father as his second-in-charge: "For even the Son of Man came not to be served but to serve, and to give his life as a ransom for many."[27]

I hesitated to include Jesus in this chapter and run the risk of reducing his life to a good example for us to follow, as in, "Be like Jesus and Joseph; don't be like Judas and Haman." The Bible does not discourage following a life worthy of emulation.[28] If we're not careful, however, "a life well lived" can replace the true gospel of "a new life in Jesus." So, let me be clear: We are all Haman and Judas—at least as bad and quite possibly worse. We are hopeless sinners apart from God's grace in the person of Jesus Christ, and apart from God's power in the person of the Holy Spirit. But in Christ, we are "holy and blameless and above reproach" and capable of doing the work God has called us to do—not because of our own competence, but because of his life at work in us.[29]

24 Matt. 24:36.
25 John 4:34.
26 John 3:16; Gal. 4:4; Eph. 1:9–10.
27 Mark 10:44–45.
28 1 Cor. 4:16.
29 Col. 1:22.

Only when we're united with God through Jesus are the examples of this chapter of any help to us. Without him, no amount of good advice, helpful illustrations, or ministry work can save us. I can't overstate that enough, and I implore you to keep the truth of the gospel (faith, not works) in mind as we move on to a few more contemporary lives we can learn from.

CHAPTER TEN

FRED ADAMS:
"JUST START SERVING"

When I first came to Mars Hill Church, our retrograde financial struc-
ture, mechanics, and policies were suited for a church of 4,000 (weekly
attendance), but we were running 12,000. As I worked through the
rebuilding process, I reached out to large churches that we respected
and could learn from in the areas of stewardship and organizational
processes. I contacted Fred Adams, executive business pastor at Harvest
Bible Chapel outside Chicago, and he was super interested in helping
us and providing great reference material.

Since that time, Fred and I have become friends, sharing many
meals and even a bowling match with our lead pastors, Mark Driscoll
and James MacDonald. A man with Pastor Fred's background and
love for the church is exactly the type of guy I hope reads this book and
decides to serve Jesus, the church, and the lead pastor.

How would you describe your role at Harvest working with Pastor James?

I oversee all financial operations and business operations of the church. We believe that good, sound business principles are what God expects in stewardship. We make sure things are done professionally and to the best of our ability. I oversee anything that has any financial component—operations, facilities, IT, our camp, our television studio, our school facilities and budget, and the fellowship—essentially all of the different aspects of ministry that the church has.

How do you handle all of those operations while still serving the lead pastor?

That's always a delicate balance. I need to be available according to James' schedule because his schedule is so intense with the ministry responsibility that he has. I need to be able to adapt my schedule to fit his. He did a multicity tour recently, so we had meetings on the road—scheduled and unscheduled, as ministry opportunities came up. There's always a need for input, to make sure things are consistent with the vision and that we're on the same page. We'll travel together occasionally, and that helps us connect because it gives us more time than a fast, hurried meeting in the office or in the hallway. Supporting the senior pastor comes in many different forms: praying, deflecting issues that don't need to get to him, making sure that he sees only the things that need his attention, and redirecting everything else.

How do you steward your influence with Pastor James? How do you facilitate the vision God has put on his heart for the entire church and avoid pushing your own agenda?

I'm a very creative person, and that's unusual for an accountant.

But I don't have the need or the vision to pursue my own ministry or my own way of doing things. I was attracted to Harvest because James has a very high view of Scripture, the gospel is proclaimed boldly, and the worship is Christ-centered and God-honoring. The passion I had for the church was developed before I came on staff. I thought, "I want to be a part of this. I want to help. I want to do what I can to advance this mission." I'm not going to put myself in God's way. I want to be used by God in a powerful way. To find a good executive pastor, I think it's really important to look for somebody who's already passionate and plugged into the church and the direction that the church is being led in. You should never become an executive pastor in hopes of changing the direction of the church. You should be excited about where the church is going and be able to say, "I can use the gifts that the Lord has given me to advance this. I can see areas where I can add energy and add expertise to benefit the overall ministry."

How did you end up working for a church?

Before I started working for the church, I was semiretired/self-employed. I didn't have to work too hard to make ends meet, so I had time to volunteer. When I first came to Harvest, I just started volunteering and making myself available in different ways, and the Lord kept opening doors. I did my part and just stepped through the doors that he opened. One thing led to another, and, before I knew it, I was on staff. Even then I continued to step into different roles. I came on as the CFO, and that position evolved into more of an executive-level role, and eventually I was responsible for all construction, all facilities, and all operations.

What were you doing before you started working for the church?
I'm a CPA, and I worked as a controller and in management information. I started my own businesses in the '90s, so I was self-employed by the time I actually came on staff. I had a business background—from carpet-cleaning to floor-contracting to general contracting, building houses, and I'm also a real estate broker. I have a real estate brokerage company, and I put various partnerships together. I've worked with rental properties, investors, and developers, including those in downtown—and that went really well. I reached a point where I was just managing the rental properties that I still had. I had time to volunteer, and the rest is history.

How did you recognize your calling to serve the church?
It's different for everybody. For me, there was no voice from the Lord, but there was a definite stirring in my heart. I thought, *I've got time to serve. I've got the ability to serve. I can see areas of need.* Serving out of your giftedness, strengths, and skill set is very rewarding. I could have served by directing cars in the parking lot—and praise God for everybody who serves in the parking lot—but for me it's not the same thing as serving in an area that I know well, like finances. Serving the Lord in the area of your highest and best use is really rewarding in terms of spiritual satisfaction, joy, and spiritual growth.

If you're wrestling with whether or not you're called, just start serving. Start doing something. You'll know, because you'll find something you want to do more of. Not that it's easy. At times it's very difficult, and it's not always fun. But it brings joy to know that the Lord is using me. I look back on my life and career, and I can see how God used those experiences as training for my executive pastor role. You talk about confirmation. There's the desire—you want to do more—and then you just keep stepping through doors, and the Lord will confirm it with you.

In 1994 I went through a business experience that was very painful. But I learned some very important lessons that I used in 2008 at Harvest, and I saw clearly why God took me through all of those difficulties back in '94. It's that confirmation combined with the desire to do more that reminds me that I'm doing what I'm supposed to be doing.

Your calling is confirmed, you're seeing fruit, and God is using you. But the dark days still come. How do you work through the hard times when you're super tired and you start thinking about all the other things that you could be doing that would be much easier?

Those days are never fun because they reveal something about my heart that I don't like to see. I see my selfishness, my desire for what I want, my self-reliance, my self-sufficiency. And usually, by the time I get to that point in the list, I break down and realize, *Yeah, I'm an idiot. I shouldn't be feeling this way.* The fact that I get to serve is such a privilege. The day that you lose sight of that privilege is the day when those bad, dark feelings can come in. The God of the universe doesn't need me to go out and do this. He can get his will done through a lot of other people. Yet he chose me. I have to constantly express both my gratitude and my excitement over the fact that I get to do this. There are plenty of talented people out there. God could have put one of them in this spot, but he put me here. Focusing on me leads me into those darker places quicker. As soon as I can get the focus off of me, things get better. It also helps to consider our place in the course of Christendom and realize, *OK, I'm not getting eaten by lions. I'm not getting sawn in two. I'm not getting beaten and shipwrecked. I'm not getting falsely accused and thrown in prison. My deal's pretty good.*

How do you and Pastor James complement each other?

I'm a more reserved, regimented process-thinker. James is creative and expressive, jumping from topic to topic. But there are so many ways in which we think exactly the same. The complementary piece comes into play in terms of skill set. I know finance and accounting, which James has no desire to do. He wants to know that we have oversight and reporting structures and that things are getting done according to his expectations, but he doesn't need to know the details. That provides an incredible amount of freedom. We need to make everything top-notch, with no irregularities, but within that box we can set systems in place to reach the objective in a very efficient way, which is where my expertise and creativity come into play.

Likewise, James describes himself as a "play baby," always looking for a chance to goof off. That's me, too. So, we connect on some personal levels, which helps because ministry can be intense.

How do you overcome growth barriers as a church?

Our only barriers are ourselves, honestly. We never focus on a number or say, "We have to be this big by that date." We focus on spiritual depth and ask, "Are people growing? Are people being fed? Are people plugged in and serving?" We look at metrics like that. In a human sense, I might care about reaching 15,000 some-day, but in a spiritual sense, I believe the Lord is going to hold us accountable for the people he has brought us. He's going to ask, "How did you steward the lives I've entrusted to you?" I want to make sure that we're not overlooking the spiritual growth of the people who are here. I'm not saying it's either/or, but our bent is to be more focused on that.

James' book *Vertical Church* is about inviting the glory of the Lord to come down into the church and allow people to see that and want that. We want that to happen every week, and we don't care what the number is necessarily. Earth-shattering, window-rattling worship service each week that honors the Lord is what we're driving at. At that point, the growth is up to the Lord. Whatever he brings our way we'll be grateful for, and we'll do our best to pour into those people and make sure they're fed.

Pastor James and Harvest have so many ministry opportunities. How do you say "no"? How do you prioritize?
We don't have it figured out perfectly. We're excited about what God is doing, and as the Lord brings opportunities, we need discernment. We have a high sense of urgency because our time is short. We talk through new ideas every week and look at the opportunities that are out there. We try and prioritize our opportunities based on what the Lord has entrusted to us, and reach the most people with it. We want to spend ourselves in ways that help.

Our 25th anniversary is coming up, so we're trying to figure out how to balance a good anniversary—thanking the Lord for his favor and blessing these past 25 years—with the other ministry needs that are going on. We really try and do that through conversation, first assessing the things that we call "big rocks" and then deciding what we're going to focus on after that.

Once you set those priorities, then you have to protect the time. You need to have the discipline to say "no" and recognize that every time you say "yes" to something, you're also saying "no" to something else. There's always all kinds of wants, needs, and requests that come across my desk, and I often have to say "no" because we've chosen to do something else instead. Be intentional about sticking to your mission, impacting the kingdom, and stewarding what God has entrusted to you.

What does ongoing growth look like for your church and for you personally?

We're always working on that next thing. By God's grace, we continue to grow, and we've got to provide for those people. I've got to be proactive in thinking about that next thing coming. I don't want to be in the spot where I've run out of seats or I didn't pay the electric bill.

Find guys at churches of a similar size and ask them questions and talk through issues. That's by far the most effective way to get information. If you're an executive pastor of a church of 500 people, find other executive pastors at churches of 500, and maybe a couple at 1,000. Talk to those guys and ask what they've done, how they've handled certain situations, and what they're currently working on. Build a trusted circle of people you can talk to, who will openly and honestly share what's going on. It's always awkward initially when you start talking to somebody new, but without disclosing genuinely confidential information, talk it through. Those are ways to get valuable pieces of information, because why learn from your own mistakes when you can learn from somebody else's?

As far as personal growth goes, obviously it starts with your personal relationship with the Lord. I'm making sure I get my daily quiet times in, that I'm grounded in prayer, and trusting in the Lord for outcomes, not in my skills and abilities.

Does it ever get any easier?

"Easy" is not a term that I would use to describe it. I don't think it ever gets any easier. I don't think it ever should. Because if it's easy, you're not doing everything you can for the Lord. You're just not pushing it.

CHAPTER ELEVEN

DAVID BRANKER: "STRUCTURE, SYSTEMS, AND THE SPIRITUAL"

In 2006 I began working on staff at Celebration Church in Texas. At the time, I was a brand-new Christian with no idea how to lead a church. I reached out to numerous executive pastors for help, and David Branker was one of the first guys to return my phone call. Not only did he return the call, he invited me to come to Jacksonville, where he was the executive pastor of Celebration Church in Jacksonville (no affiliation with the church I was serving).

David was a longtime executive for American Express before God called him out of the business world to serve the church. We have remained in touch over the years, and he often comes to mind. I pray for him and text him frequently. In 2011, when I started at Mars Hill Church, Pastor David graciously traveled to Seattle all the way from Florida and visited seven Mars Hill locations in two days with me. He shared with our team some really great insights.

To this day, Pastor David remains a good, godly friend whom I can always call for prayer and advice.

How would you define the role of executive pastor?

Whether it's one very special individual or a team of people sharing the responsibilities, at the end of the day, I would argue that the role is an essential component of a healthy church. Given that the role of the lead pastor is usually best focused on three or four major functions, including visionary, principal communicator, and culture creator, each of which carries a significant burden, the executive pastor should typically lead in a fashion that serves two distinct audiences well: the lead pastor and the church organization.

Before I describe the specifics of the role, I want to offer some perspective. The local church has a double nature: it is an organism (that has life) and an organization (that has structure, governance, financial framework). Within this nature, there are three essential components of a local church: (1) structure, (2) systems (or programming), and (3) the spiritual life of the church. The executive pastor role serves all three of these components:

1. *Structure* refers to the unseen reinforcements of the church, much like a skeleton. It must be sound and dependable. It includes things like financial policies and structures, facilities and their operations, and a carefully selected team of staff and volunteers who love God and love the house in which they have been planted.
2. *Systems* represent all that the church does, such as planning, programming, and your specific approach to reaching and developing fully devoted followers of Jesus Christ. It includes dynamic weekend services, small

groups, and other targeted ministries of the church. These systems reflect the unique culture and DNA of your local church.

3. *Spiritual* is perhaps the most important. It's one thing to build a building or hire a team; it's another to fulfill a sacred purpose. The church is designed to meet each week to worship God and encounter his presence, hear a message rooted in his Word, and develop an unrelenting devotion to Jesus' mission.

The executive pastor leads the development of effective structures that frame the church. He guides the formation of the supporting systems, explaining the *why* behind the *what*, measuring the *what*, and coaching the staff and volunteer teams on the *how* so that progress can be made and momentum can be maintained. He also serves as a guardian of the culture alongside the lead pastor, eliminating distractions to the work of the Holy Spirit, which he does by modeling, coaching, and mentoring through culture drift. Depending on the preferred style of the lead pastor or church, the executive pastor may focus on different emphases, yet he understands that the structure must always serve the systems, and the systems must always yield to the work and leading of the Holy Spirit. Essentially, the goal is for wins to be celebrated.

How do you persevere when the work gets especially difficult?
When you realize that the sovereign God called you into a role, that for you becomes a sacred call. One of my favorite authors, Ravi Zacharias, once said, "The sacredness isn't in what you have been called into but in the fact that you have been called." Knowing that the sovereign God placed this assignment before me was all

the evidence I needed to know that he would help me navigate the highs and lows that came with it.

How do you rest in God? Can you provide any practical examples of what Sabbath looks like for you on a weekly and annual basis? Resting in God—this is something I failed miserably at. There are many vices in the human heart. Not building in times for rest was one of those I seemed to justify most often in the name of ministry.

As a recovering ministry-holic, I have since realized that my issues were twofold: first, not allowing myself the needed breaks, and second—perhaps more dangerous—poor energy management. Even when I had time off, I found myself thinking and daydreaming about things I needed to do, problems that still needed to be resolved, and opportunities waiting to be seized. Even though I wasn't in the office, my thinking and energy were divided. I started to manage time off as a religious activity, rather than fully disengaging when appropriate so that I could engage in other priorities.

For years, I would come home after a long day, spend time with the family, and after everyone had gone to bed, I would turn on the computer and work on emails, ministry plans, and even sermons. I have had to embrace the reality that I needed to be a better steward of my body—which means rest. Though I have made some progress in this area, I would not claim total victory at this point. But progress has been steady.

Rest and energy management are two keys to sustained health. It starts with rest—getting our required daily hours of sleep and taking a day off each week (i.e., a real Sabbath where we are not involved in creating or generating work). It also means scheduling vacation time, even if we are not going out of town. Energy management is more difficult to address. I have discovered that the latter is multidimensional. It can be physical, emotional, and also spiritual in nature. Understanding what energizes you and those things that drain you are key to managing energy. For example, we are all physically energized through some combination of rest and exercise (for me, it's more rest than exercise). Whereas, I am emotionally energized in my quiet time and in journaling my thoughts, others are energized emotionally by spending time with people they enjoy. But most importantly, as spiritual beings, we are designed to draw our energy and build our strength through waiting upon God and seeking his face daily. As the prophet Isaiah reminds us,

"But they that wait upon the Lord shall renew their
strength; they shall mount up with wings as eagles;
they shall run, and not be weary; and they shall walk,
and not faint" (Isaiah 40:31, KJV).

There is a huge difference between self-motivated striving and moving in the grace that God has given you. When we choose to wait upon the Lord, we defer to following the Father's pace over our own. It is no surprise that Jesus only did what the Father asked him to do. Perhaps there's an important principle here in finding our own grace rhythm.

In addition, it's important to recognize that we were designed to flourish within boundaries in every dimension of our lives. God is unbounded, but we are meant to thrive within boundaries, trusting fully in him. For example, God is not limited by time, but we are. You and I have been given a limited number of hours in each day and limited energy. Therefore we must prioritize how we expend our time and our energy. On an emotional level, my wife and sons need my best energy, not what's left over at the end of a grueling day of meetings. So developing a rhythm and pace that can be sustained is key.

On a practical level, managing energy also means not saying "yes" to every meeting and not participating in every decision. Energy management is a great catalyst for empowering others who are well able to make the decision. There are a few other practical changes I made to be a better manager of my time and energy:

- I started to do more thorough preparation work for meetings. I would think through meetings ahead of time and try to mentally process what progress would look like at the end of each discussion. Having a plan going in minimizes meeting drift.

- I recognized when the task at hand could not be completed in a day and determined ahead of time how much progress I would be satisfied with. It's always better to make a little progress every day than to try to make exhausting monumental leaps—even though I love monumental leaps. Who doesn't?

- With my family time, I've shifted from just praying together to spending a few minutes in a devotional as a family each evening. This has been a huge lift. There is nothing more fulfilling than discussing the Bible with your kids; many times their perspective can be very enriching to you personally.

- I now take the difficult step to shut down my smart phone when I am home, and I remove the telephone from our dinner table entirely. I discovered that even in vibrate mode, though I wasn't answering the phone anymore, my thinking would immediately shift to wondering who or what may be in need of my attention.

Learning to acknowledge our limits and fully trusting and drawing from the one who is limitless is what keeps us sharp in ministry. It's also what gives us a leading edge. Isn't it just like God to equip us for success in what he has commissioned us to do?

How do you capture your lead pastor's vision? How do you re-communicate that vision to others?

I have been privileged to serve under multiple gifted lead pastors, most recently Stovall Weems at Celebration Church. He is one of the most visionary leaders you will ever meet. The first thing I had to come to terms with was realizing that my vision or prior church's vision had to be fully surrendered. We all have a propensity to remember the past better than it was, and so it was important to intentionally let go of past ideas, in order to understand the needs and perspectives of the lead pastor I was now serving. My role was to serve my lead pastor's vision, and I found great contentment in that.

In the executive pastor role, you are a steward of another's vision, but that does not mean you no longer have differing ideas. When the time was appropriate, I would share ideas, though I would never lobby for them. Whether or not they were received wasn't my burden to carry. My role was first servant and steward, not primary decision maker. There were actually times when my pastor incorporated my ideas in vision statements, but even then, I never shared them as if they were mine. Why? They weren't. I had the privilege of playing a small part in a vision way bigger than me. I discovered that there is great satisfaction when you give the best of yourself to a cause greater than yourself, and there is no greater cause than the local church. Since God is the one who entrusted me to serve in his house, when he births creative ideas in and through me, it is important for me to remember that the ideas were never mine to begin with. They all belong to the Father, for his use, and he is the one who appointed my pastor as the author of the vision.

Here are some simple, yet practical, techniques I've used to capture and relate my lead pastor's vision:

- Listen and use his words. Language is important. In communicating the vision, use his language, his examples, his illustrations, etc. You are another voice to the same vision; your job is not to try and improve on it.
- Watch out for areas where people are having difficulty synthesizing the vision, and build better bridges to help them feel it, understand it, and recognize it. For example, find stories or testimonies of life change that encapsulated the fruit of the vision, and share those at the beginning of team and volunteer meetings.
- Enthusiasm. You cannot sell something you are not enthusiastic about. If you feel you have a better idea, that will undermine your enthusiasm and the integrity with which you can share the vision.
- Pray and ask God for creative ways to display the vision. I use matrices, charts, and pictures. Incorporate points into the message. That makes it easy to keep it in focus and in front of the team.
- Celebrate the wins and ensure every team has a win that is aligned with the vision.
- Eliminate systems and programming that undermine the integrity of the vision, even if the system or program is established and seemingly successful.

Beyond these steps, it's important to have a compass that drives the reason you do what you do. For me, it was the responsibility of stewarding something that is sacred—that is, the good news of the gospel. You see, when we settle for mediocrity in the way we communicate the good news of the gospel, we undermine the treasure and importance of its message.

A sacred and treasured message demands our very best in the way it's communicated and in the way we present it each week at our local churches.

CHAPTER TWELVE

DAVID CHRZAN: "JESUS ABOVE ALL"

As the friendship between Pastor Mark Driscoll and Pastor Rick Warren has grown, I've been privileged to get to know David Chrzan (pronounced "Shawn"), Saddleback Church's chief of staff. I really appreciate the friendship and love that David demonstrates for Rick Warren. Their relationship has served as the example for the sort of relationships I want to encourage between the lead pastors and executive pastors of Mars Hill Church.

Pastor David operates on the next level of leadership, and he has offered tons of counsel to me and Mars Hill. Even though he is super busy helping to lead a massive church, he has always been quick to reply with great, encouraging, and much appreciated advice.

How did you get into ministry?

Fifteen years ago, before I came to Saddleback, I was pursuing ministry by going to seminary. I lost everything I owned in a fire, and then I almost lost my wife and family in a separation. I moved from Texas to California and got a low-end job. I lost that and then joined the sheriff's department, where I was a law enforcement officer for about ten years. During that time, I went back to school and got my master's degree in organizational management. Before I finished my degree, one of the pastors at Saddleback asked me to put together a training program for some of their leaders. A few years after that, he called me and asked me to come on staff and work with him. I did, and I came in as a guy who was helping other people get mobilized and volunteer in the church. About fifteen months later, Rick Warren came down to my office and asked if I would help him directly. September 9, 2001, is when I started working with Rick.

What are some of the major milestones and turning points that stand out over the years?

Any reinvention always involves outside pressures and inside pressures. There are outside expectations (i.e., things that need to be done), and there are inside barriers (i.e., your own skill, capacity, and identity issues—your own insecurities).

When I first started working for Rick, he went into a six-month period of seclusion where all he did was write for twelve hours a day. I was facilitating a lot of stuff that Rick wanted done, with him being completely and utterly out of the pocket. There were other leaders leading the church, but I was the go-to. At the time, I was nothing more than a glorified executive assistant. I was a one-man crew. But because Rick was so out of the pocket, he started giving me big things to do. He would give me these long lists of things to do. For the first three weeks, the items were usually something as simple as getting his prescriptions, picking up his clothes, or making sure that an e-mail gets written—very assistant-based things. Then the list started to change. As I would get things done, Rick had trust in what I was doing, and he started adding bigger things. For example, he wanted to do a weekend where people would renew their wedding vows, complete with wedding cake and wedding photos for everybody. So I moved from project doer to project manager. The more I managed projects, the bigger the projects got. Soon, I transitioned to leading bigger areas of the church where I wasn't just doing projects anymore.

I went from being task-focused to project-focused within a standard of values, and then I went on to lead bigger things with leadership values. It was an ongoing progression. Each progression meant that I had to work with more staff and more volunteers. I went from being a single person with no staff—but I brought in twenty volunteers. Then I got one staff, and we multiplied to sixty volunteers. Then I got two staff, and we went to two hundred volunteers. I just continually built this infrastructure under me so that the more Rick gave me, the more I got done.

Along the way, I built relationships with all of the leaders and helped them get their jobs done, and that's kind of what led to my role today. I'm chief of staff. I'm an executive leader, but I'm not *the* executive pastor. I'm like the chief of staff at the White House in that there's no way that the five-star general of the army is going to take orders from me. I bring him to the table and facilitate directions from the commander in chief. I do have leadership influence, and I do have leadership credibility, but philosophically and functionally, I've received that because of the way I've tried to serve these guys and the way I've supported them.

How do you get vision from Pastor Rick?

We let him give it. He presents the vision, and once he's done, everybody around the table has an idea of what their part is in that vision, either based on the past or their area of expertise. My role becomes important when Rick moves on to the next thing and the staff has to come back for questions. I'm more available than Rick. Once the vision is out and done, when people have questions, when things aren't working out, or when it's unclear who's supposed to do what, I come in to fix things and do the problem solving.

Rick will sit down and share his vision, and then once he's out and everybody is asking what it means for them, I call the meetings and work through all of the dynamics of making it happen.

How have you managed to focus on Jesus and make time with him a priority?

It's a constant struggle. I have to be fully focused on what I'm doing in that moment. I don't get to turn off my phone, but I do get to take vacations. I do get to spend time with my kids, watch them play soccer, and all of those things. When I spend time with Jesus, I know that I have to focus in that moment. I can't say that I prioritize it; it's just the focus. I'm not assured that I'm going to get time with Jesus every morning at six o'clock. My life doesn't work that way. I wish it did, but it doesn't.

For one thing, I've not been able to wake up and dive into Scripture first thing. Sometimes I don't believe in God until nine o'clock in the morning. My body may be up, but that doesn't mean that anything else is going on. I have to cherish the moments that I get when I get them. I don't have a real structured life in that regard. I have to be available to so many people because I serve them, and I don't get to set the times of when their problems take place. I can't schedule when people die. It's kind of like working in a fire department: some days are great, and I've got plenty of time, and I don't have a lot to do; other times, man, we're all over the place.

How do you avoid turning your ministry into a job?
First of all, you have to believe it's a calling and not a job. When you start thinking in terms of how the world defines a job, now your heart can be changed by a few extra dollars here, a corner office there, a nametag on the window, and that kind of stuff. You can get completely sucked into that, and so one of the things I say not only to my staff but also to my family is this: just because you have a privilege presented to you doesn't mean you should take it. You may think that you should have the front parking spot because you're one of the top leaders. The other leaders, staff, and elders may even say you should take it. But that doesn't mean you should. Your calling is not the accoutrements of what you get; your calling is to serve. I've shaped my circumstances and my behavior to say, "I'm serving." I park 150 yards away from the office to keep my space open for volunteers. I still drive a used car because I don't need a big flashy car, and I don't want people to see me that way.

How did God call you, and how have you endured the difficult seasons that come with the territory?
When my wife and I just about separated, I wanted to be a senior pastor of a church. I wanted to be in full-time Christian ministry at the front of the church. And it didn't happen. Two days after we separated, my wife called and said, "Either you give up the idea of going into ministry, or I'm not coming back."

That rocked me. After about a month of working through that, I said, "Look, I wanted to go into ministry, but I want to go into it with my family, the family that I've got." So I pushed pause on that calling. But for the next six years, every time my wife and I talked about ministry—even if it was just serving in the church—we fought. The very first journal entry that I wrote, probably in 1993, said, *God, I can't continue to live the way I am right now. I can't continue having my heart, desire, and passion in ministry without my wife there to support me or be behind it. I don't care what you have to do, just please either take away this call or do something with it, because I can't live like this.*

Within eight months, God did a miracle in my wife's life. She became my biggest cheerleader to get back into ministry. Ironically, by that time I had already said, "I'm done. The timing's not right. I'm not worried about it, so 'Get thee behind me.'" I pushed away from it. So my wife got my small group in on it. And for the next four years, my small group hounded me, and God chipped away at my salary. Six years after that, the door opened for me to step back into ministry.

You have to acclimate to your calling one way or another. Pastor Mark Driscoll didn't become a pastor of a church of 15,000 on day two. He couldn't have handled it. But he's grown through the seasons to the point where he's acclimated to it. Acclimation is difficult because you have to gain confidence. Even if you're always confident in what God is calling you to, you still have to learn new skills and get comfortable using those skills. And then at the next level up, you have to learn new skills again. You have to acknowledge that there is a grieving process at every step of growth. When you first get to a certain level, you'll probably start pulling your hair out and get overwhelmed. But then you stop and say, "OK. What are we going to do about it?"

Today, I take my family along with me and we serve together. My kids were asked early on, "Your dad's away from home a lot.

He has to travel a lot. He's always in the public eye. How do you feel about that?" They would say, "Well, that's our dad, and that's the way God has shaped him." My family has seen my gifting, and they understand.

As you interact with these influential leaders, how do you guard your heart against pushing your own agenda and your own projects above what God has called Pastor Rick to do?
Up until recently, I didn't "own" anything besides Rick's agenda. Then about three years ago, leadership put me over all communications. Communications was a direct extension of Rick's voice. At that point, I became a principal in decision making rather than a facilitator, because now I had to speak into things and ask for budget. The agenda I had was trying to extend and enhance Rick's voice. More recently, I was able to raise up leaders to take on communications, so I'm back to the place where I don't own anything except what Rick wants done.

If you're an executive pastor and you have your own agenda, you're always going to be at odds internally with yourself and you're always going to be at odds with the organization. If you're going to want to do your thing, you won't have time to do the right thing for the organization. Three things have helped me with this:

1. Value staff above myself.
2. Value church above staff.
3. Keep Jesus above all.

I serve the staff above myself, but I don't allow the staff to limit my ability to serve the church. That is, if I have to move staff out or change staff, I decide based on what benefits the church, not what benefits the staff. And then, it's Jesus above all.

CONCLUSION

THIS BOOK EXISTS FOR ONE REASON

We all invest our lives in something or someone (e.g., money, hobbies, possessions, career, achievements, ourselves, family, etc.). From one business-savvy brother to another, the best investment decision you can make is investing your gifts for Jesus' mission by serving him, his church, and a lead pastor.

Thank you for picking up this book and considering how God might use it to lead you and speak into your life. I pray that the Holy Spirit has helped you see the role of executive pastor in a different light and opened your heart to some new "investment opportunities" for the remaining days, years, and life which God has entrusted to you.

As I wrote this book, many people told me that I needed to change the content in order to reach a broader audience and sell more copies. But I did not write this book to sell copies. I wrote this book so that more men might be called to lead as executive pastors, serving Jesus, serving their church, and serving their lead pastor.

If this book encourages just a handful of executives to leave the business ranks and become full-time executive pastors, I consider it a success. If a few lead pastors read this book and catch a vision for how an executive pastor could help them reach and serve more people for Jesus, I consider it a success. If a couple of dozen business guys respond by serving their church as volunteer executive pastors, I consider it a success.

I pray God uses this simple book for such an achievement, for the good of his church and through his faithfulness at work in you.

Diagnostics for Prospective Executive Pastors

20 THINGS TO LOOK FOR IN A RIGHT-HAND MAN

WHEN IT COMES to the calling of leadership, there's nothing wrong with being #2.

In fact, it's a high calling. For instance, Jesus is the right-hand man of his Father (in fact, seated at God's right hand), having done the work God the Father sent him to do.

A good right-hand man is hard to find. The following is a list of thoughts I recently sent to the Mars Hill Church lead pastors, fourteen men who lead each of our local churches, whom I love very much and want to have good godly support for. It consists of what to look for in their second-in-charge. These thoughts are in no particular order, and I thought it might be helpful to pass them on. A good right-hand man is someone who does the following:

1. Prays for you and your family often

He's the one guy who, you can guarantee, will pray for you if you ask him to, and he prays for you and your family every day.

2. Loves you

He sees himself as your ally on mission, is for you, and wants you to succeed.

3. Does your thing

He's not using you to do his thing.

4. Goes where you go

If you are teaching a class, he is there with you. If you have a meeting, he's there with you. He's there to help you, see what you see, learn, listen, assist, encourage, and give you feedback by asking good questions on how to implement the vision God has given you.

5. Honors you

Particularly in front of others, he sets a culture of respect by referring to you as his pastor and genuinely respects your spiritual authority.

6. Tells you the truth

If it's bad news, he tells you privately and respectfully, and he gives you the truth in love.

7. Complements you

He knows what you aren't good at, and he does those things so that you can do what you are good at.

8. Works in the church so that you can work on the church

He does a lot of day-to-day leadership tasks so that you can fig-ure out the future—e.g., how to serve more people, reach more people, and train more leaders.

9. Gives you the information you need in a regular and organized fashion

For me, this is a Tuesday and Friday lengthy "items e-mail" that takes me an hour or more to read and respond to. All of our senior leaders give organized information, and the executive pastor organizes it into one document so that I know everything that is going on, can answer any questions, and speak into any issues by responding to one long e-mail.

10. Is humble enough to act like an assistant when needed

If this means you need something to eat, a cup of coffee, or an errand done, he's willing to do it as needed.

11. Does not manipulate his access to you to get special treatment

He's not trying to squeeze in excess pay, an ear for his pet projects, friends, or more.

12. Prays a ton

He prays for you, the church, and pretty much anything and everything.

13. Loves Jesus and the church more than he loves you

Both are hugely important. If he only loves Jesus, he will not serve the church. If he only loves the church, it becomes an idol replace-ment for Jesus.

14. Gets stuff done

If you give him a task, you don't have to follow up to see if it's done. If you find that you aren't giving a task because you do not trust him, he needs to change or he's not a good fit.

15. Is always accessible

If you call or text on his day off, he's available and on it.

16. Is enjoyable

You will spend enough time together that, if not "friends," you at least enjoy one another, have some laughs, and are brothers.

17. Works hard

He pulls the hours to get the job done. You simply don't wonder if he's dogging it.

18. Does not want your job

He's not trying to leverage his job to get something better and is content to do his job so that you can do yours.

19. Is not greedy

He does not manipulate expenses and reimbursements to take advantage of his position.

20. Is faithful to the end

If the time comes for him to move on, you know you can kindly ask him and he will do so without dropping the ball, being divisive, or going into attack mode, because he loves Jesus, the church, and you.

Originally published on theResurgence.com.

HOW TO FIND AN EXECUTIVE PASTOR

HERE ARE SOME basic tips for lead pastors and churches in search of a good executive pastor, presented in no particular order:

1. Look for a guy who has run a staff and managed a budget—small business owners, restaurant managers, and anyone who has done well working in a high-stress environment with limited resources.

2. Don't settle for any general "business guy." Brokers, insurance salesmen, and financial planners may seem like the right fit, but many people working in these fields don't know how to manage people or budgets.

3. Résumés may look better with big companies listed on them, but big companies can sometimes be a place to

hide. A numbers cruncher at Microsoft can say they've worked at Microsoft, but that doesn't mean they have any practical leadership experience.

4. Anyone who has ever started a business will understand the practical aspects of church-planting, such as how to make due without any money or staff. It may be difficult, however, for really strong entrepreneurs to follow another leader's vision, which is a necessary attribute of an executive pastor.

5. If you're interviewing the right kind of people, you'll be talking to folks who have wrestled with the idols of money, position, and status. There's a chance some of your candidates still worship these gods, and if so, they won't last long working for a church. The low pay, long hours, and zero glory will leave him looking for "another calling."

6. If you interview candidates working at other churches, be sure to ask, "Does your lead pastor know we are talking today?" If the answer is "no," run away. If you hire them, chances are they'll go behind your back someday as well. Equally discouraging is when a candidate assures me they'll give their church two weeks' notice. Their current church needs more than two weeks to ensure a good transition. That's not a healthy transition plan, nor is it the perspective of someone who cares about the church. They're just looking for the next job opportunity.

7. Remember that the right fit for the role depends on the strengths and skills of the lead pastor, not just the qualifications of the executive pastor. "The importance of complementary skills means that second chairs are not interchangeable parts."[1]

8. Make 100 percent sure that the candidate's wife feels called, too. She must be excited for the church to use her husband's gifts, even if it means low wages and long hours. If the family is not on board, the disconnect will cause problems down the road.

---

1 Bonem and Patterson, *Leading from the Second Chair*, 37.

WHAT IS AN EXECUTIVE PASTOR?

Serve Jesus. Serve your church. Serve your lead pastor.

THIS SIMPLE JOB description defines the role of the executive pastor. At Mars Hill, the executive pastor (XP) is the second hire we make for any new local church, after the lead pastor. Together, these two men complement each other to form the core of an effective church leadership team.

The lead pastor focuses on teaching, training leaders, and casting the vision. The executive pastor focuses on systems, management, and implementing the vision. Here are ten attributes of a good XP:

1. An XP's purpose is to spread the gospel and grow the church. An XP loves to see lives changed by Jesus.

2. An XP serves.
He focuses on the success, needs, and experience of others.

3. An XP puts his lead pastor's success above his own.
If the lead pastor is doing his job well, the church will grow and expand (see #1).

4. An XP handles all of the day-to-day operations of the church.
An XP must know how to run a business in order to ensure good stewardship of church resources and finances. His responsibilities also include all of the logistics for weekly services and other events.

5. An XP reinvents himself.
Depending on the characteristics and needs of the lead pastor, and depending on the size of the church, an XP must adapt over time in order to serve effectively.

6. An XP offers solutions.
An XP never presents a problem without at least one possible solution.

7. An XP covers the weaknesses of his lead pastor.
An XP knows what his lead pastor does and does not like to do. By covering the areas where a lead pastor is weak, an XP allows the lead pastor to operate out of his strengths.

8. An XP is not an assistant.
An assistant helps the lead pastor get his projects done while an XP actually completes more projects for the lead pastor, taking those projects off his plate. At the same time, an XP is not too proud to

work on menial tasks. He'll make the coffee, if necessary, in order to serve his lead pastor.

9. An XP loves second place.

A good XP is not a successor. He serves the lead pastor and doesn't use him as a stepping-stone. Though it may not always be easy, the XP gladly submits himself to the vision and leadership of the lead pastor.

10. An XP prays.

Outside of his family, nobody knows a lead pastor's struggles, stressors, and schedule better than his second-in-charge, which gives the XP a special responsibility to intercede.

Scripture sums it up best, with Hebrews 13:17–18 describing well the calling of an XP:

> Obey your leaders and submit to them, for they are keeping watch over your souls, as those who will have to give an account. Let them do this with joy and not with groaning, for that would be of no advantage to you. Pray for us, for we are sure that we have a clear conscience, desiring to act honorably in all things.

Originally published on http://theresurgence.com/2012/06/21/what -is-an-executive-pastor.